Arriving at the Test Centre

Arrive at the Test Centre about 10 minutes before the scheduled time for your test..

Park in a safe place, not too close to any other parked cars or obstructions. If there is a car park, back into the space so that when you start off, you will be facing forward and can move away easily.

Don't go into the waiting-room until five minutes before your test.............

Spend the last 5 minutes with your instructor.....

In the waiting-room ⟶

True or False

Try to relax, Remember that the examiner is a trained professional. He knows that you are nervous and inexperienced and does not expect you to do everything perfectly. He only wants to make sure that you can drive safely to a reasonable standard, following the rules of the road....

In the Waiting-Room

Are You Ready For Your Driving Test?

Mike Nathenson

Illustrated by Janet Nunn

endorsed by
The British School of Motoring

Pan Books
London, Sydney and Auckland

About this book

The book begins on the morning of the day you take your test and leads you, step-by-step, to your meeting with the Examiner at the Test Centre.

It gives you practical, useful advice on
* What preparations to take at home
* What to do one hour before the test
* Where and how to park your car at the Test Centre
* What to do in the Examiner's waiting room
* What to expect from the Examiner before you reach your car

It then moves on to the Driving Test itself. As the person being tested, you sit beside the Examiner in your car and drive around busy high streets, town roads, suburban lanes, dual carriageways and roundabouts – following traffic signs, making turns, starting on hills, meeting pedestrians approaching level crossings, etc. in short, meeting every conceivable situation you could meet on the day of the test.

The Driving Test ends back at the Test Centre where the Examiner asks you a series of questions on the Highway Code.

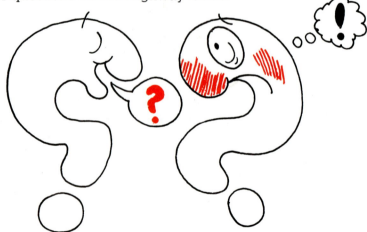

All the information in the book is presented in a simple lively way that gets you actively involved right from the start.

···· and how it works

Driving situations on the left-hand side of the page and questions about the situations on the right-hand side.

The answers to the questions appear at the back of the book. If a question is answered incorrectly, you are not only shown the correct answer, but also where and *why* you went wrong. The answers have exactly the same form as the questions, so you can see at a glance whether you are right or wrong and why.

At the very end of the book, there is a Driving Test Score Card. You use it to add up your scores and answer the one all important question: "Am I ready for my driving test?"

The day of the Test (do's and dont's)

Eat a good breakfast. Don't go to the driving-test on an empty stomach →

If it's winter, dress warmly, (you may have to open your window for arm-signals) Wear a heavy, loose jumper — not a bulky coat → to give you plenty of room to move your arms during manoeuvres.

Wear a comfortable pair of shoes that will not slip off the pedals. Wellingtons and other heavy boots, or stiletto heels which might jam under the brake-pedal — are OUT!

If you wear glasses or contact-lenses — put them on!
— and - GATHER YOUR DOCUMENTS TOGETHER

Your valid provisional driving licence signed in ink.

An up-to-date insurance certificate that qualifies you to drive the car in which you are taking the test!

A valid M.O.T. certificate (if your car is over 3 yrs old.)

These documents should be with you whenever you drive·······

Check over your car.

Our Test is being taken in a regularly checked, and well-maintained B.S.M. Austin metro _ but if you are using your own car, remember to go through the same checks that B. S. M. do, and make sure that.....

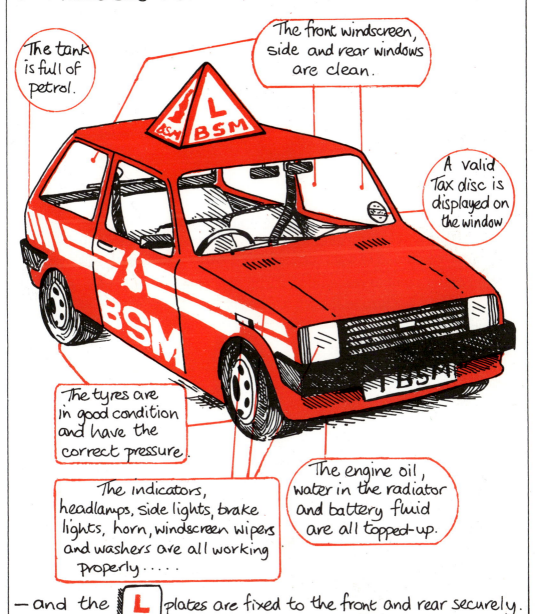

The tank is full of petrol.

The front windscreen, side and rear windows are clean.

A valid Tax disc is displayed on the window

The tyres are in good condition and have the correct pressure.

The indicators, headlamps, side lights, brake lights, horn, windscreen wipers and washers are all working properly.....

The engine oil, water in the radiator and battery fluid are all topped-up.

— and the L plates are fixed to the front and rear securely.

One hour before the Test

Arrange a lesson with your instructor. The purpose of this last lesson is to make sure that you are mentally ready for the test.

It should be a lesson that "simulates" a real driving test. Your instructor should play the role of the examiner sitting beside you. He should give you directions and tell you when to do a manoeuvre.

The aim is to put you in the right frame of mind for the test by relieving a lot of your nervousness in advance. It will also give you a good idea about what the *real* test will be like in one hour's time. The lesson should last about 30 minutes. Ask your instructor to meet you one hour before the time of your test. Make sure you have all your documents plus a copy of *The Highway Code* and the booklet *Your Driving Test*. Drive to the Test Centre. On the way, ask your instructor to plan a route suitable for practising the emergency stop, the turn in the road and the reverse into the side road. The route should also include any difficult hazards in the general vicinity of the Test Centre like, for example, an awkward one-way system, a dangerous crossroad, a tight turning into a narrow road, etc.

The important point to remember during this final lesson is to *relax*. If you hit the kerb on the turn in the road, don't worry. Try it again. Getting it right now will give you added confidence during the test.

Pre-driving check

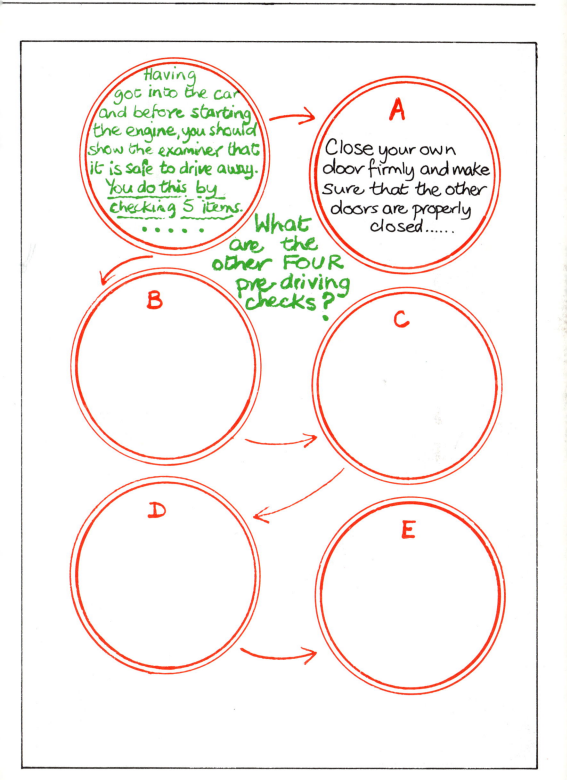

Having got into the car and before starting the engine, you should show the examiner that it is safe to drive away. You do this by checking 5 items. . . . . .

A

Close your own door firmly and make sure that the other doors are properly closed......

What are the other FOUR pre-driving checks?

B

C

D

E

Moving off from rest

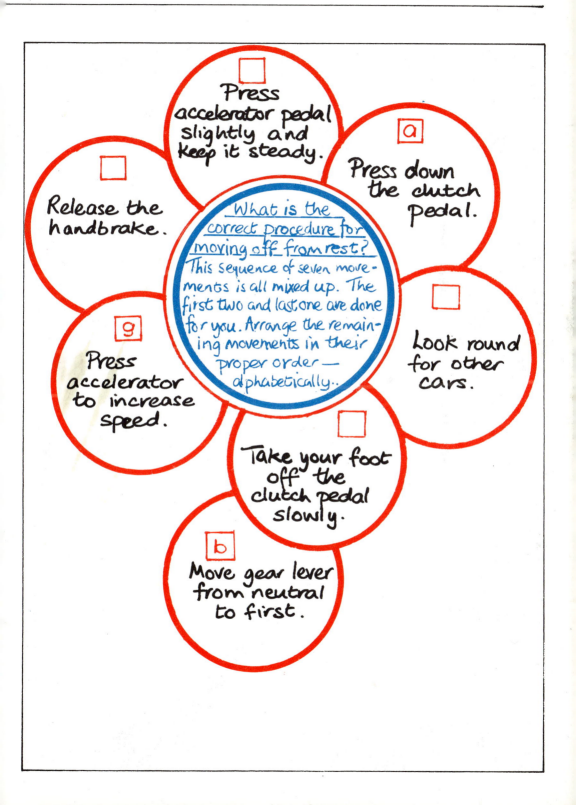

☐ Press accelerator pedal slightly and keep it steady.

a Press down the clutch pedal.

☐ Release the handbrake.

What is the correct procedure for moving off from rest? This sequence of seven movements is all mixed up. The first two and last one are done for you. Arrange the remaining movements in their proper order — alphabetically..

g Press accelerator to increase speed.

☐ Look round for other cars.

☐ Take your foot off the clutch pedal slowly.

b Move gear lever from neutral to first.

The Stop sign

b. You should only enter the main road when you can do so without causing danger or making drivers on that road change speed or direction.
T ☐ F ☐

c. The two solid lines at the end of the road are there to warn you that you are approaching a main road with traffic moving in both directions.
T ☐ F ☐

a. Giving a signal, getting into the correct position, and adjusting your speed — are all essential to the right-hand turn.....
T ☐ F ☐

Are these statements. TRUE or FALSE? Place a tick in the appropriate box.

d. You should check your mirror and then look to the left, to see if there is a gap in the traffic, before emerging.
T ☐ F ☐

e. When it is safe to emerge you should move off smoothly and begin your turn immediately after passing the centre of the road.
T ☐ F ☐

Stopping behind a parked car

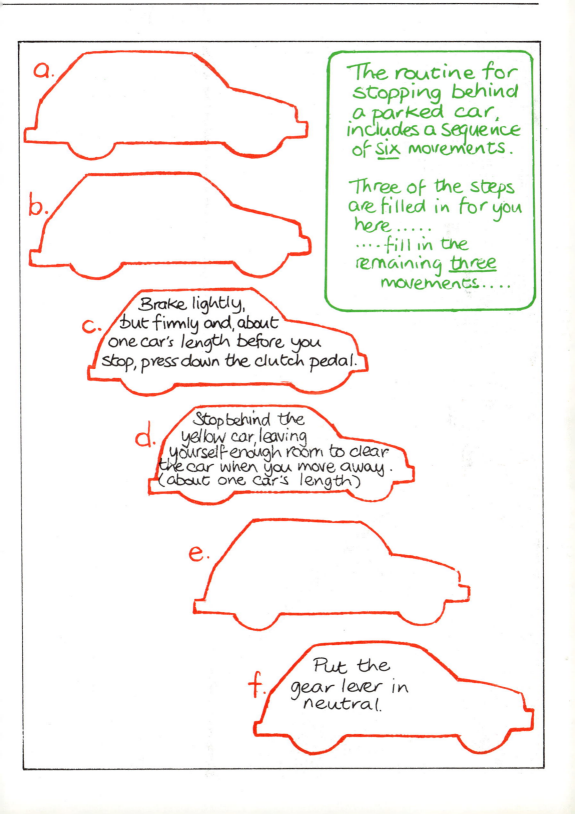

a.

b.

The routine for stopping behind a parked car, includes a sequence of six movements.

Three of the steps are filled in for you here......
.....fill in the remaining three movements....

c. Brake lightly, but firmly and, about one car's length before you stop, press down the clutch pedal.

d. Stop behind the yellow car, leaving yourself enough room to clear the car when you move away. (about one car's length)

e.

f. Put the gear lever in neutral.

Moving away at an angle

Questions

Answer the following 4 questions in the spaces provided.

? a. What is the examiner looking for when he asks you to do this manoeuvre?

b. What two observational checks should you make before moving off?

! c. There are two additional dangers that could occur in this situation —

What are they?

1.

2.

d. How should you warn other vehicles that you intend to move off?

Traffic-light signals

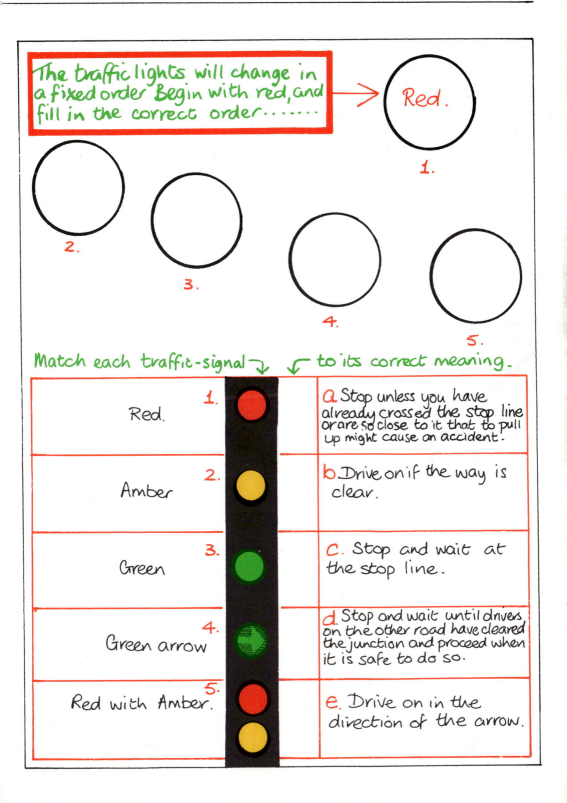

The traffic lights will change in a fixed order. Begin with red, and fill in the correct order.......

Red.

1.

2.

3.

4.

5.

Match each traffic-signal to its correct meaning.

Red.	1. 🔴	a. Stop unless you have already crossed the stop line or are so close to it that to pull up might cause an accident.
Amber	2. 🟡	b. Drive on if the way is clear.
Green	3. 🟢	c. Stop and wait at the stop line.
Green arrow	4. 🟢	d. Stop and wait until drivers on the other road have cleared the junction and proceed when it is safe to do so.
Red with Amber.	5. 🔴🟡	e. Drive on in the direction of the arrow.

Turning left in a busy area

Overtaking a parked lorry

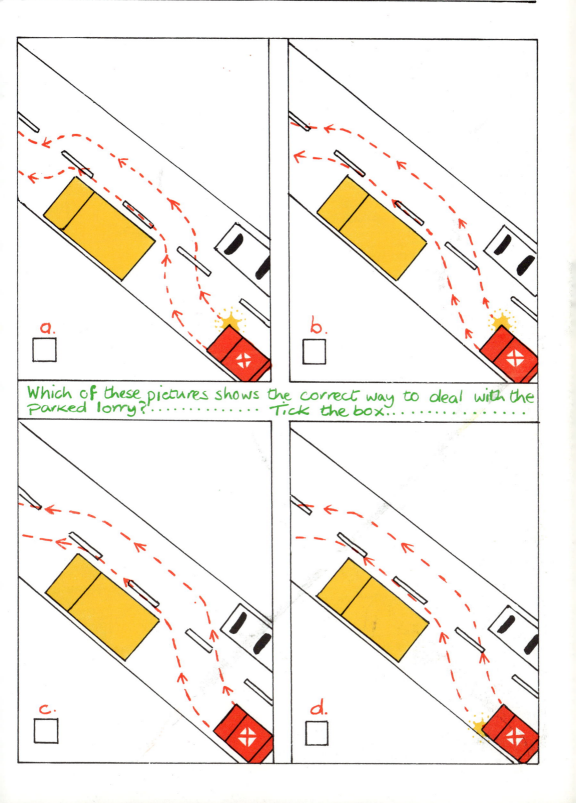

a.

b.

Which of these pictures shows the correct way to deal with the parked lorry?............... Tick the box.................

c.

d.

Turning right at a roundabout

The Emergency Stop

Are these statements TRUE or FALSE ?
Place a tick in the appropriate circle .....

a You should look in your mirror before you stop, to make sure that a car isn't following too closely.

T ◯ F ◯

b You should signal left to warn other drivers.

T ◯ F ◯

c You should gradually increase the pressure on the brake as you slow down, instead of stamping on it.

T ◯ F ◯

d Having started to brake, you should then depress the clutch pedal to help you stop.

T ◯ F ◯

e You should keep both hands on the steering-wheel until the car has stopped.

T ◯ F ◯

f You should apply the handbrake just before you stop.

T ◯ F ◯

g The amount of brake pressure you should apply depends upon the state of the road-surface.

T ◯ F ◯

Parking for the reverse

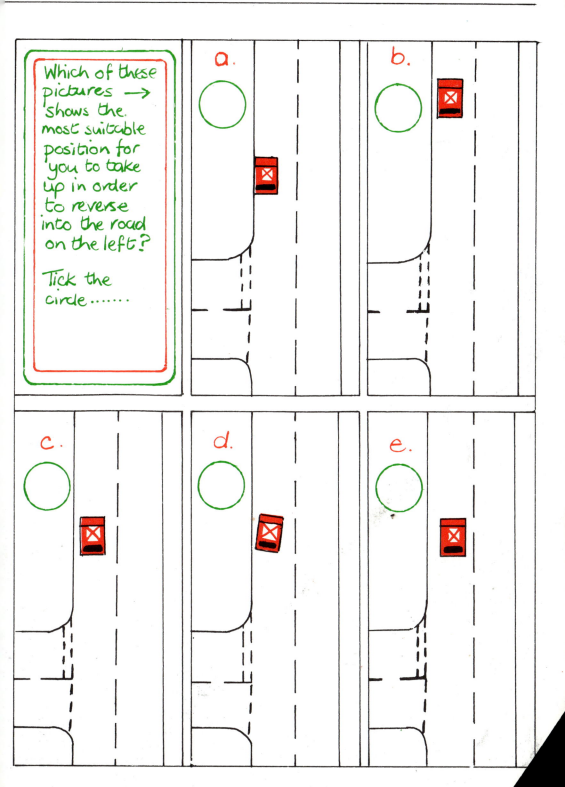

Which of these pictures → shows the most suitable position for you to take up in order to reverse into the road on the left?

Tick the circle......

a.

b.

c.

d.

e.

Reversing around a corner

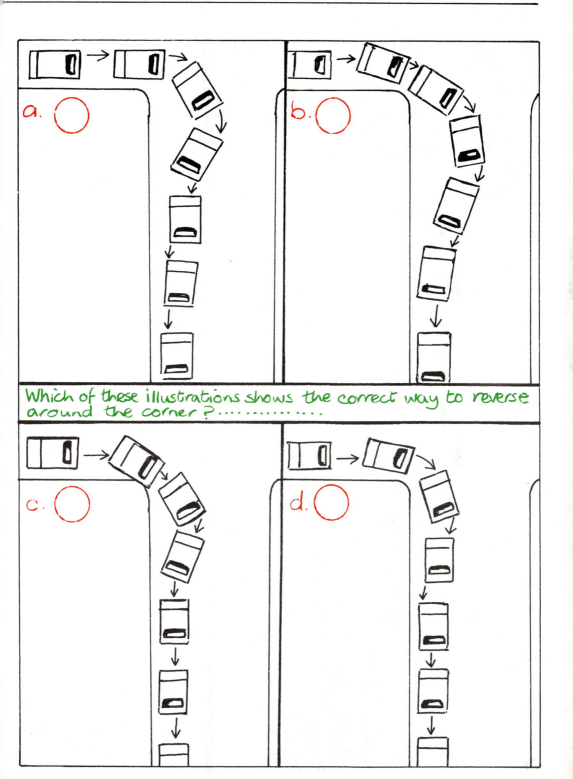

a. ◯

b. ◯

Which of these illustrations shows the correct way to reverse around the corner? ....

c. ◯

d. ◯

Turning left (after reverse)

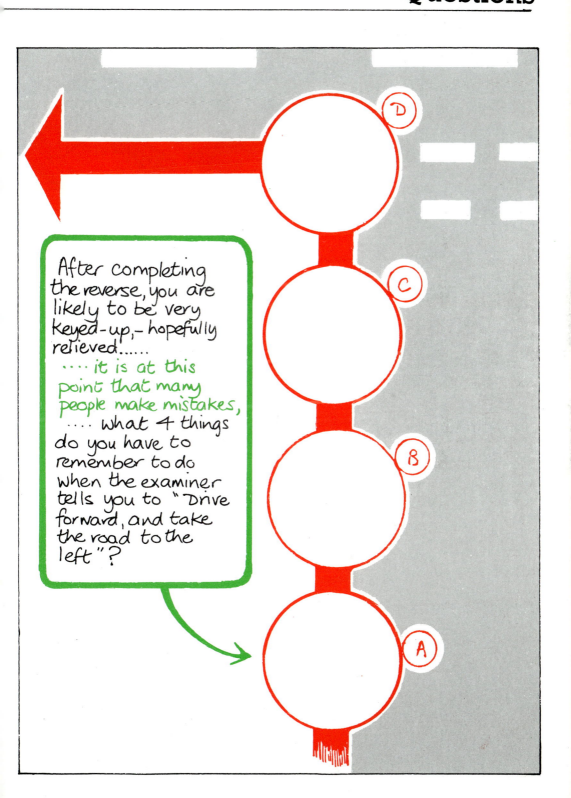

Judging a safe gap between cars

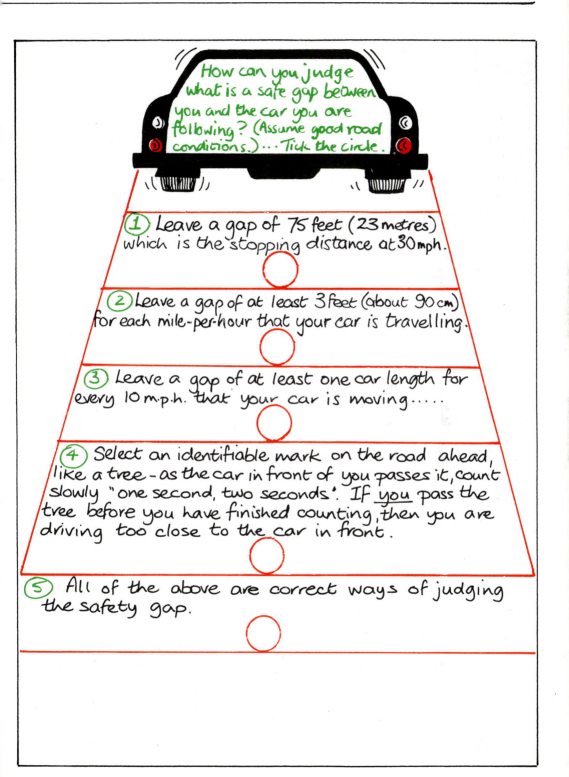

How can you judge what is a safe gap between you and the car you are following? (Assume good road conditions.)... Tick the circle.

1 Leave a gap of 75 feet (23 metres) which is the stopping distance at 30 mph.

2 Leave a gap of at least 3 feet (about 90 cm) for each mile-per-hour that your car is travelling.

3 Leave a gap of at least one car length for every 10 m.p.h. that your car is moving.....

4 Select an identifiable mark on the road ahead, like a tree - as the car in front of you passes it, count slowly "one second, two seconds". If _you_ pass the tree before you have finished counting, then you are driving too close to the car in front.

5 All of the above are correct ways of judging the safety gap.

Judging your stopping distance

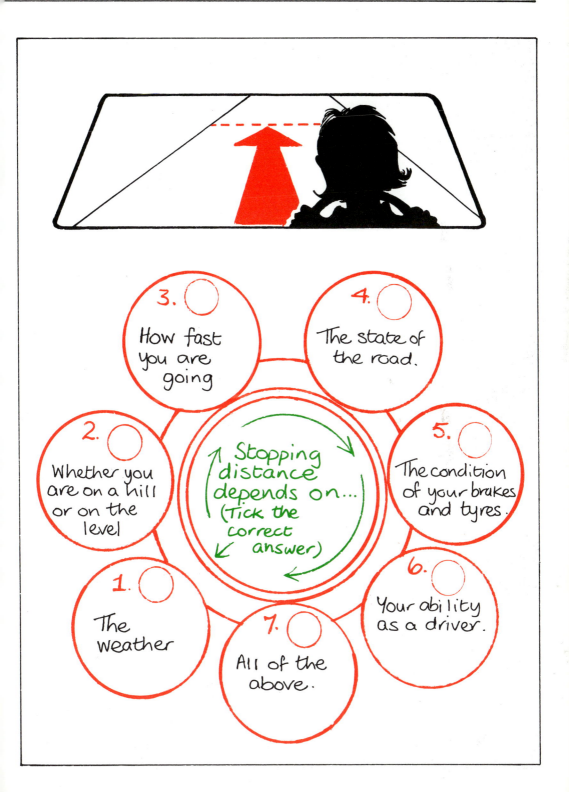

Overtaking parked cars

The examiner will not tell you whether it is safe to overtake the parked cars. You must show him by your actions that you can handle the situation properly by choosing the right time and place for overtaking.

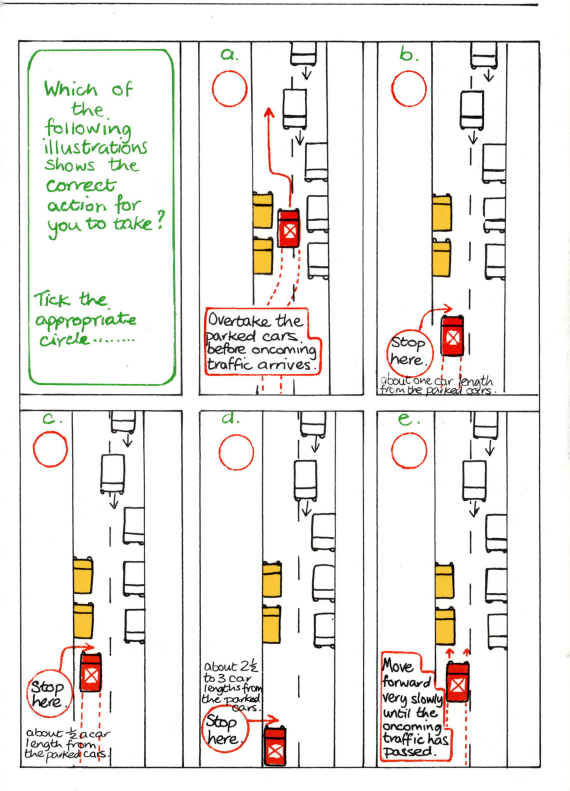

Going uphill

Are these statements

TRUE or FALSE?

Place a tick in the appropriate circle.

a The warning sign tells you how steep the hill is.
T   F

b. The higher the percentage on the sign, the steeper the hill— e.g. 15% is steeper than 14%.
T   F

c. Try to stay in a high gear as you climb the hill, because changing down can cause a loss of speed and acceleration.
T   F

d. Keep well back from the van in front of you, so that you do not need to make a sudden stop.
T   F

e. Overtaking uphill is a much more difficult and dangerous manoeuvre than overtaking on the level.
T   F

15%

Stopping on hills

Place an X on the picture to show the most convenient place to stop.

Remember that you are parking on a hill and your car will be slower in pulling away than if it was on level ground, so, be sure to select a place to stop that allows you maximum visibility of the road behind and ahead of you. You will need a larger gap in the traffic in order to move off safely.

Remember also, not to park too close to any obstructions. Your car might roll back when you move off .....

FARE STAGE

BUS STOP

Moving off uphill

Fill in the blanks below with the correct words.

(a) The main difference between starting off uphill and on the level road is that slightly more _____ is necessary on the hill start.

(b) Because your car will be slower in moving away uphill and gaining speed than on the level, you will need to find a larger ____ ___ ____ ____ if you are to fit in safely.

(c) If your handbrake is released before the clutch is at the point of contact, then the car will ____ _____

(d) It is important not to bring the clutch up any higher than the point of contact because your car would try to move forward before you release the handbrake and you would_____

(e) Before moving off remember to:
(i) _____
(ii) _____
(iii) _____
(iv) _____
(v) _____

Going downhill

(a) When going downhill, you will have more difficulty slowing down the car by braking, than if you were travelling on a level road. ○ T ○ F

(b) When going downhill, if you depress the clutch, your car will lose speed. ○ T ○ F

(c) For safety reasons, it is important to select the right gear before beginning to go downhill. ○ T ○ F

(d) When travelling downhill the use of low gear will help you to reduce speed by giving you more braking power and control. ○ T ○ F

(e) In general, the steeper the gradient of the hill, the higher the gear you should use. ○ T ○ F

Are these statements TRUE or FALSE?

Place a tick in the appropriate circle.

Approaching a pedestrian crossing

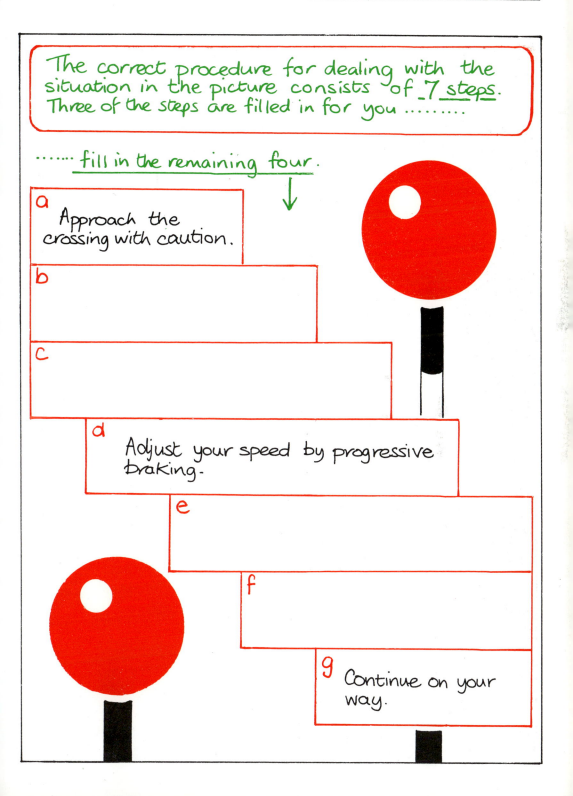

The correct procedure for dealing with the situation in the picture consists of _7 steps_. Three of the steps are filled in for you ....

.... _fill in the remaining four._

a   Approach the crossing with caution.

b

c

d   Adjust your speed by progressive braking.

e

f

g   Continue on your way.

Parking for turning in the road

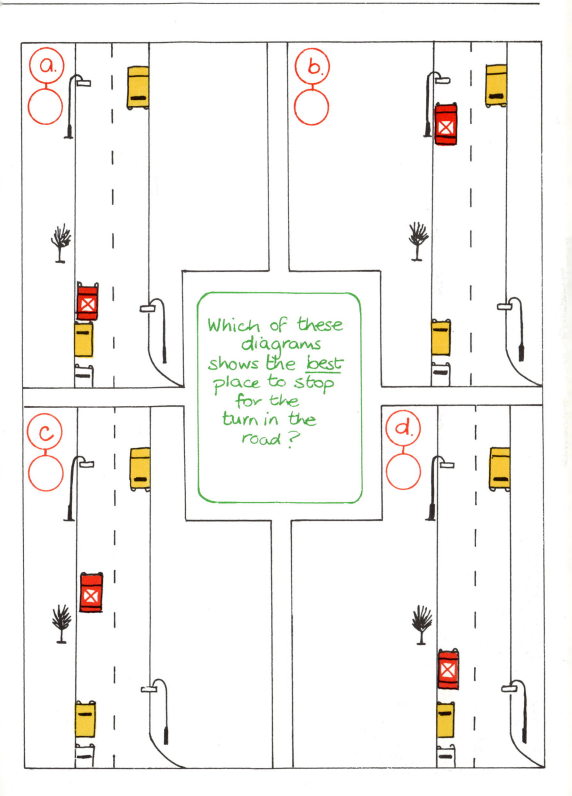

Which of these diagrams shows the best place to stop for the turn in the road?

Turning in the road

The correct procedure for turning in the road, includes a sequence of 9 steps. The first part of each step is given below. Complete each step by describing the correct actions you would take.......

a Select first gear, press the accelerator lightly, and release the —————.

b Make sure that it is safe to move off by checking ① ————— ② —————
③ ————— ④ —————

c Bring the clutch up slowly until the car begins to move and then steer quickly and fully—————.

d When you're over the centre of the road, push the clutch down, steer to the left and, when you are near to the kerb, —————.

e Remembering that the car will be on a slope, prepare for moving back across the road in the same way as you would prepare the car for a —————

f Check that it is safe to move back across the road, by ① looking right, left, and over your left shoulder for pedestrians, ② prepare the car for moving off by balancing the car on the clutch and releasing the handbrake, ③ then do your observations by: —————

g When the car begins to move, —————.

h When you're over the centre of the road, push the clutch down, ————— and when you are near to the kerb, gently brake to stop.

i Prepare the car for moving forward by
① looking in your mirror
② looking right, left, and right again.
③ looking at the road ahead, slowly move forward to a —————

Making progress to suit road conditions

Making progress to suit varying road conditions is a very common point for test failure.
Each of the following TRUE/FALSE questions deals with a different aspect of making progress.

Tick the correct dial.

a. During your driving-test you must never go over 30 m.p.h, even in higher speed limit areas.

T F

b. If road and weather conditions are good, and the speed limit is 30 m.p.h. you should try to be travelling at about 28mph in fourth gear as soon as possible.

T F

c. In the picture, you should drive smoothly up to 30 m.p.h., selecting fourth gear as soon as it is practical.

T F

d. If you come to a 40 m.p.h. speed limit during your test, and the car ahead is travelling at about 40 m.p.h., you should not increase your speed, but rather continue at about 28-30 m.p.h.

T F

e. Travelling at 25-30 m.p.h. is always safe.

T F

Approaching crossroads

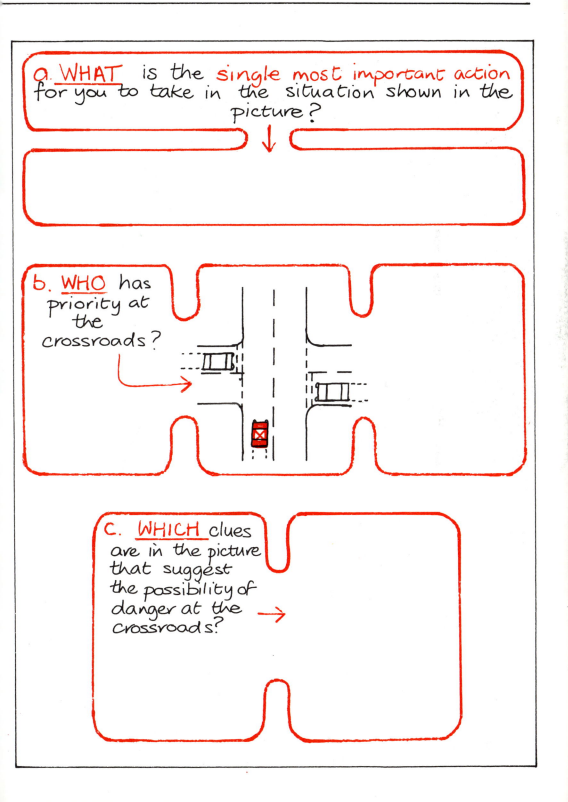

a. **WHAT** is the single most important action for you to take in the situation shown in the picture?

b. **WHO** has priority at the crossroads?

c. **WHICH** clues are in the picture that suggest the possibility of danger at the crossroads?

A dangerous situation

There are
3 potential dangers
in the situation shown in
the picture.
What are they?

1.

2.

3.

The Double Bend

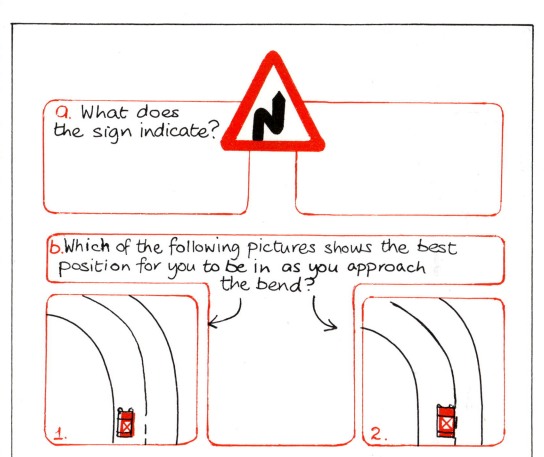

a. What does the sign indicate?

b. Which of the following pictures shows the best position for you to be in as you approach the bend?

1.

2.

c. What do the 2 continuous white lines on the bend mean? →

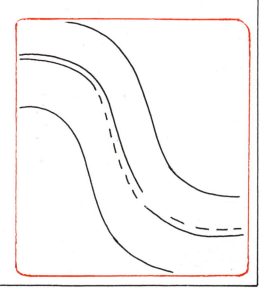

d. What do the broken lines between the 2 bends indicate?

Level crossing – half-barriers

a. What do the amber lights and flashing red lights mean?

b. What will happen within seconds when the red lights begin to flash?

c. What should you do when the barriers come down?

d What should you do if you are crossing the tracks and you hear the bells begin to ring?

e. What should you do if you stall on the crossing?

Give-way sign at a T-junction

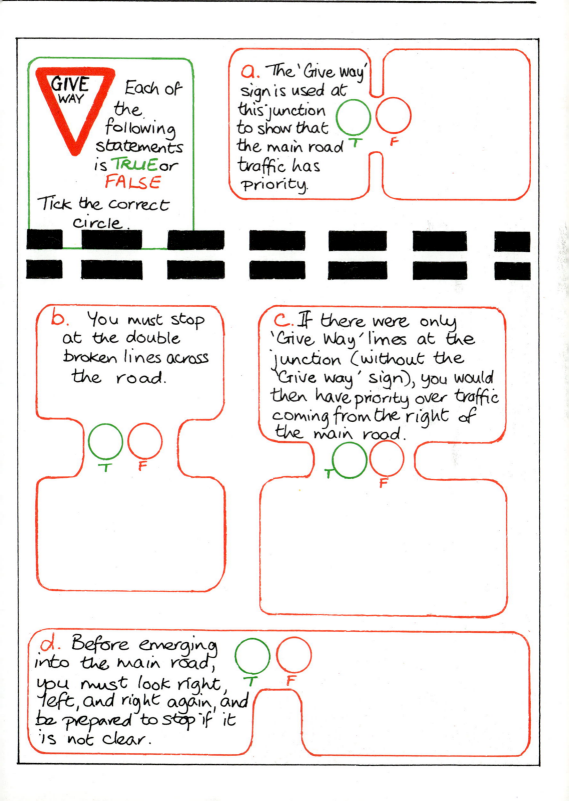

GIVE WAY

Each of the following statements is TRUE or FALSE

Tick the correct circle.

a. The 'Give way' sign is used at this junction to show that the main road traffic has priority.

T F

b. You must stop at the double broken lines across the road.

T F

c. If there were only 'Give Way' lines at the junction (without the 'Give way' sign), you would then have priority over traffic coming from the right of the main road.

T F

d. Before emerging into the main road, you must look right, left, and right again, and be prepared to stop if it is not clear.

T F

The staggered junction

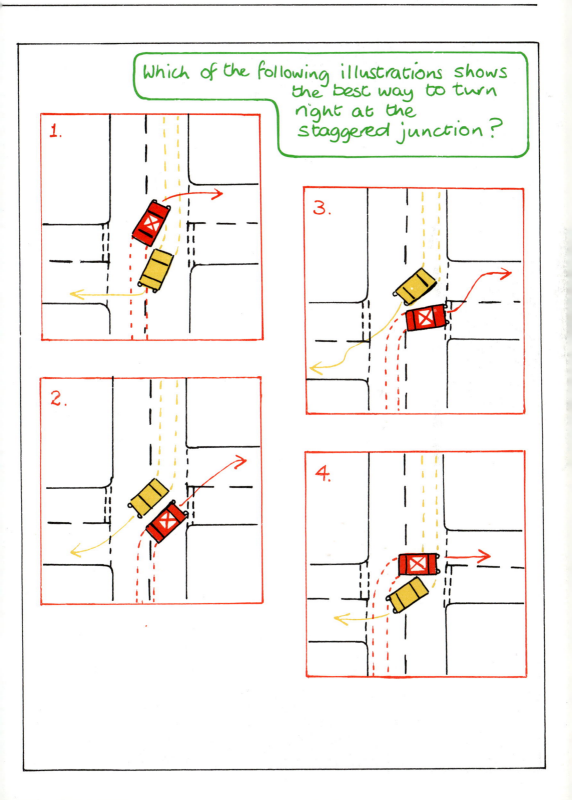

Straight on at a roundabout

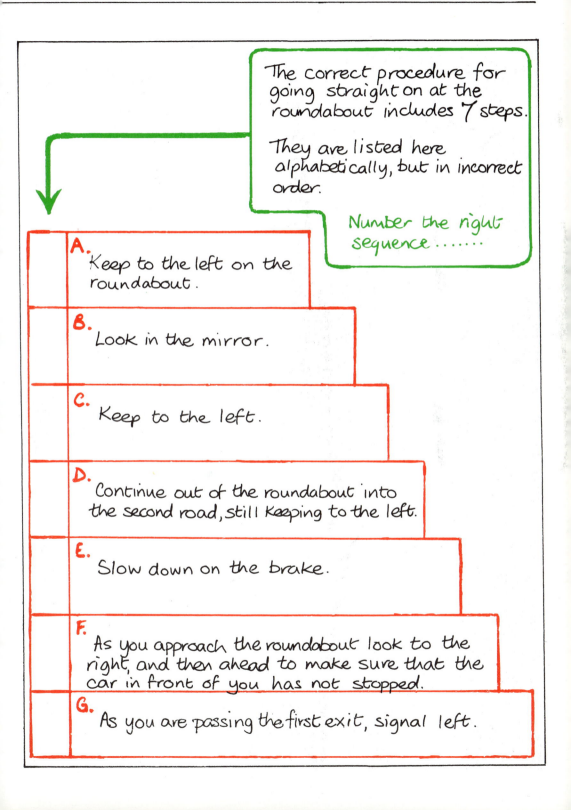

The correct procedure for going straight on at the roundabout includes 7 steps.

They are listed here alphabetically, but in incorrect order.

Number the right sequence.......

A. Keep to the left on the roundabout.

B. Look in the mirror.

C. Keep to the left.

D. Continue out of the roundabout into the second road, still keeping to the left.

E. Slow down on the brake.

F. As you approach the roundabout look to the right, and then ahead to make sure that the car in front of you has not stopped.

G. As you are passing the first exit, signal left.

Turning right off a dual carriageway

The procedure for turning right off the dual carriageway includes 5 steps.

Each of the steps listed here is either right or wrong. For each wrong statement, I want you to spot the mistake and correct it.

The first one is done for you...

A → ✗ Look in the mirror and slow down.

Should be?

✓ Look in the mirror *without* slowing down

B → Signal right only when it is safe to move over to the right-hand lane.

Should be?

C → Move over to the right-hand lane when you are about 10 feet (3 metres) from the junction.

Should be?

D → Slow down by braking and change to a lower gear ready for your turn.

Should be?

E ↓ When you reach the central reservation, turn your indicator off and wait until it is safe to make your turn.

Should be?

The One-way street

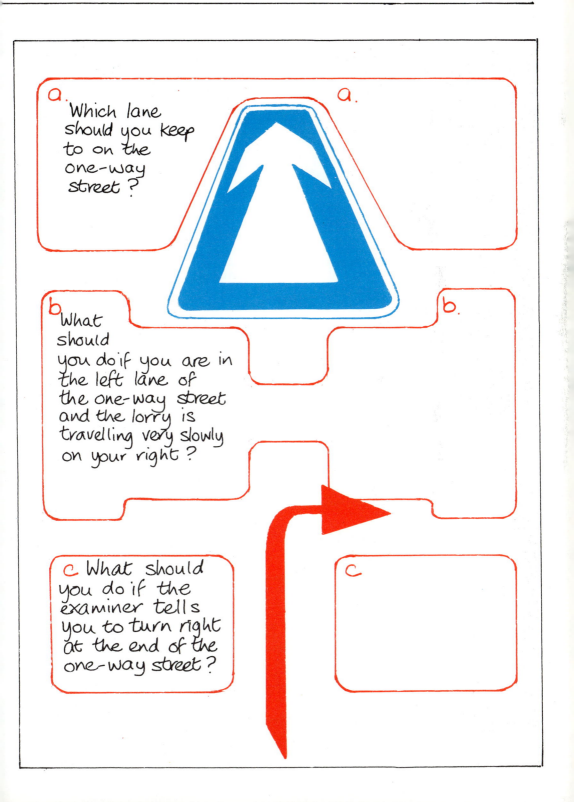

a. Which lane should you keep to on the one-way street?

a.

b. What should you do if you are in the left lane of the one-way street and the lorry is travelling very slowly on your right?

b.

c. What should you do if the examiner tells you to turn right at the end of the one-way street?

c.

Green filter traffic-lights

a
Stop and wait at the stop-line until the main light changes from red to red and amber.

b
Stop and wait at the stop-line until the main light is green.

What should you do when you get to the lights? (Assume they have not changed) Tick the correct circle ...

e
Stop at the filter arrow until you are sure it is safe to proceed.

c
Turn left without stopping if it is safe to do so.

d
Stop briefly at the lights, look left, ahead, and right, before turning left.

The pelican-crossing

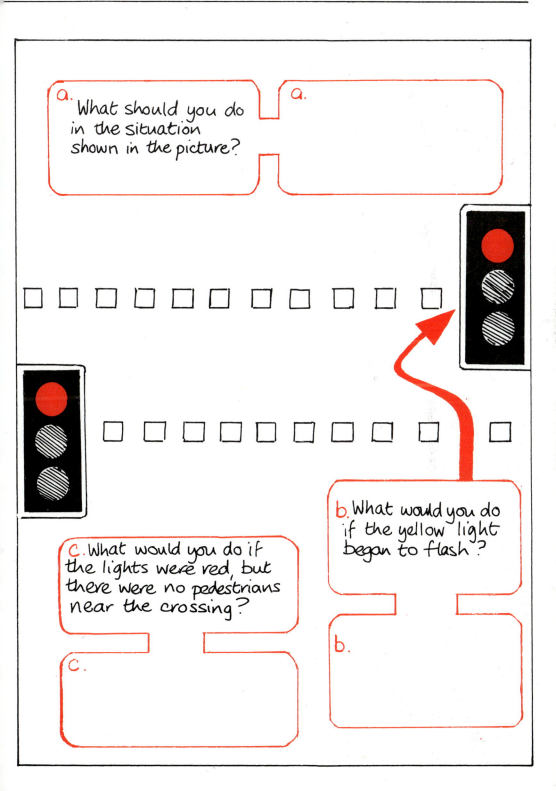

a. What should you do in the situation shown in the picture?

a.

b. What would you do if the yellow light began to flash?

b.

c. What would you do if the lights were red, but there were no pedestrians near the crossing?

c.

The Box-junction

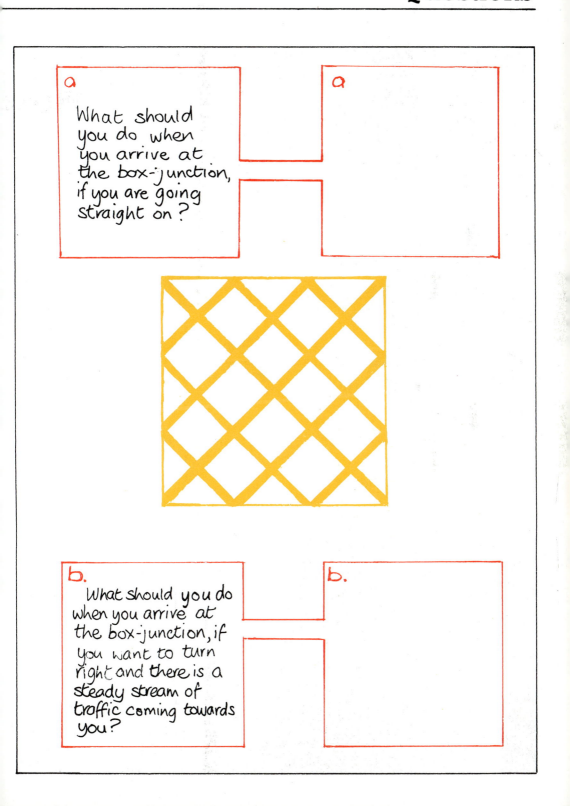

a

What should you do when you arrive at the box-junction, if you are going straight on?

a

b.

What should you do when you arrive at the box-junction, if you want to turn right and there is a steady stream of traffic coming towards you?

b.

The mini-roundabout

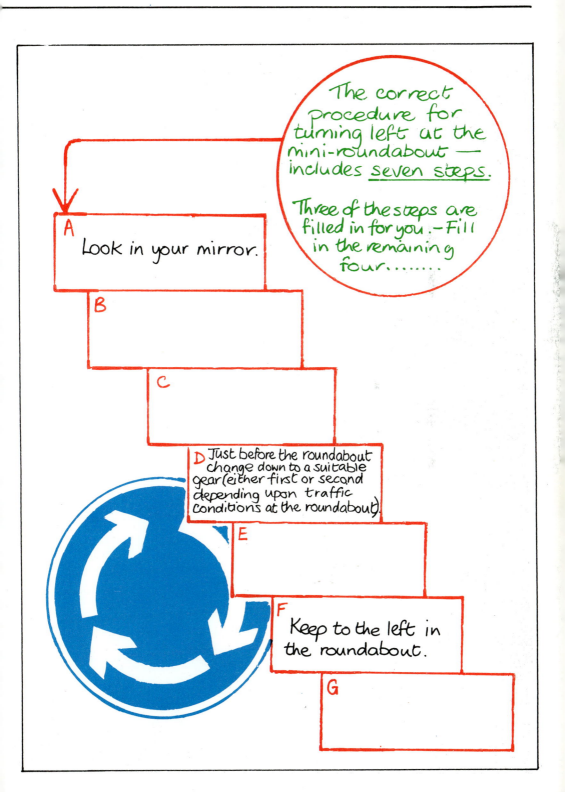

The correct procedure for turning left at the mini-roundabout — includes <u>seven steps.</u>

Three of the steps are filled in for you. — Fill in the remaining four........

A Look in your mirror.

B

C

D Just before the roundabout change down to a suitable gear (either first or second depending upon traffic conditions at the roundabout).

E

F Keep to the left in the roundabout.

G

Stopping behind a bus

Place an X on the picture to show the best place for you to stop behind the bus while it is unloading passengers.

Remember— the bus may be stopped for a few minutes before moving off.

Turning right (from a major to minor road)

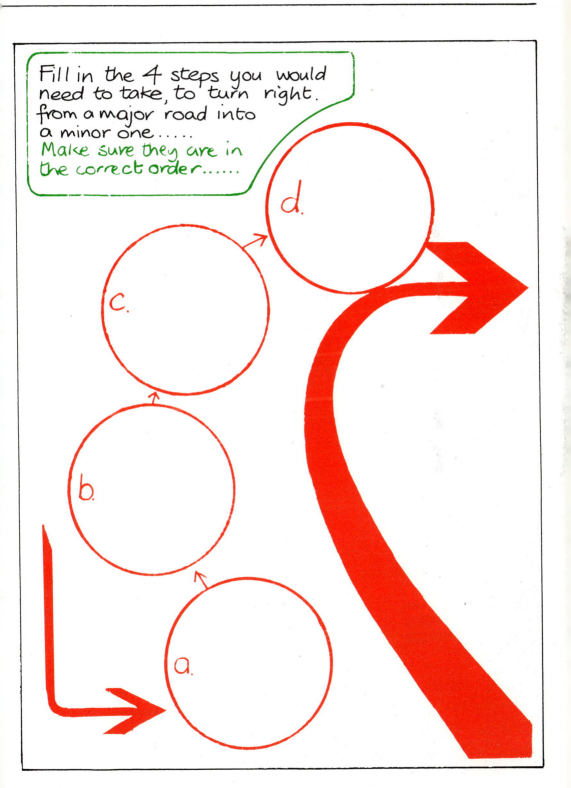

Parking in a limited space

The correct procedure for parking in a limited space between two cars includes a series of seven steps. They are all given below, but in a mixed-up order. Re-arrange them in the correct order alphabetically. The <u>first two</u> steps and the <u>last one</u> are done for you..... Fill in the remaining four.

○ When the front of your car has cleared the rear of the forward parked car turn the wheel briskly to the right.

Ⓖ If necessary move forward to straighten up.

Ⓐ Stop your car when your rear bumper is halfway along the front car and about 3 feet (90cm) out from it.

○ Continue reversing slowly and straighten your wheel as necessary.

○ Aim for the nearside front corner of the rear parked car.

○ Reverse until you are alongside the front car, and then steer left.

Ⓑ Before reversing look all around you to make sure it is safe.

The end of the road

– and the Verbal Test

At this stage of your test, the examiner will ask you about 6 questions on the Highway Code. The purpose of these questions is to test your understanding of the rules specified in the Highway Code, and your general knowledge of driving. Don't be put off by the examiner not telling you whether your answers are right or wrong. He does not expect a 100% score. He does expect you to give commonsense answers to show your understanding of the Highway Code. Usually, but not always, the questions will be in three specific areas.

a.

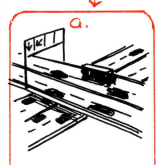

Types of roads that you haven't been driving on during the test. (e.g. motorways)

B.

Conditions different from those you have experienced during the test. (e.g. driving in the fog, on icy roads, at night, etc..)

c.

Traffic signs taken from the Highway Code.

I have prepared three sets of six questions each, to test your understanding of the Highway Code

You will find these on the following three pages, starred in order of difficulty.

*   Easy →

**   Average →

***   Difficult. →

Choose <u>one</u> of the sets and answer the questions .....

Highway Code Questions

1. Assume you are driving on a three-lane motorway at 70 m.p.h. and there are no other vehicles near you. Which lane should you be in?

2. What is the meaning of a red warning sign (a reflecting triangle) placed on the road?

3. What should you do if you are travelling along a country road during the day, and you enter a fog?

4. Under what circumstances should you flash your head-lamps?

5. What do these traffic signs mean?

a.

b.

c.

6. What do these traffic signs mean?

a.

b.

c.

Set II ------------------------- * *

1. Which lane on the motorway is the acceleration-lane?

2. What is the ideal distance for stopping behind another car at a stop-sign?

3. What should you do if you are travelling along a dual carriageway during the daytime and it begins to rain very heavily?

4. When is it an offence to sound your horn?

5. What do these traffic-signs mean?

a.

b.

c.

6. What do these traffic-signs mean?

a.

b.

c.

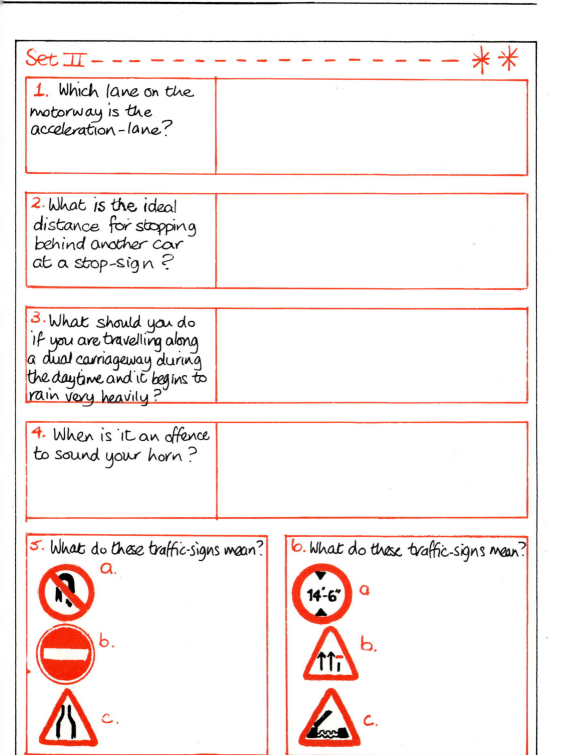

Highway Code Questions

Set III— — — — — — — — — — — — — — — — ✳ ✳ ✳

1. When driving on a motorway at night, you will see — (a) amber coloured studs. (b) red studs (c) green studs.—What does each type of coloured stud mean?

2. What should you do if you are travelling downhill on a single-track road and a car is approaching up-hill?

3. Can you name two causes of skidding?

4. When are you permitted to use a hazard-warning device? (ie. the switch which causes all of your indicators to flash at the same time).

5. What do these traffic signs mean?

a.

b.

c.

6. What do these traffic signs mean?

a.

b.

c.

—and NOW

You've completed your driving-test!!

The Examiner will now tell you whether you have passed or failed your test.....

  — but....

— since, for the moment,

THIS BOOK IS YOUR EXAMINER

you will have to find out for yourself whether you have passed or failed.

Turn the page to have a quick reminder of your test-route. then check all *your* answers

THE CORRECT ANSWERS BEGIN ON PAGE 98→

As you check each one, enter your score (ie. the number right or wrong) on the DRIVER'S SCORE CARD, which you will find on the last answer page.

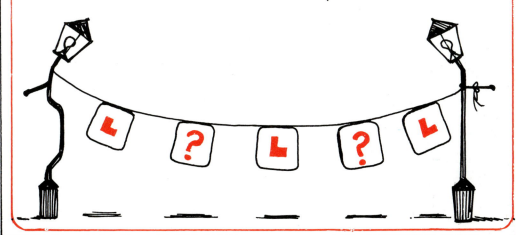

Your driving-test route

Pre-driving check

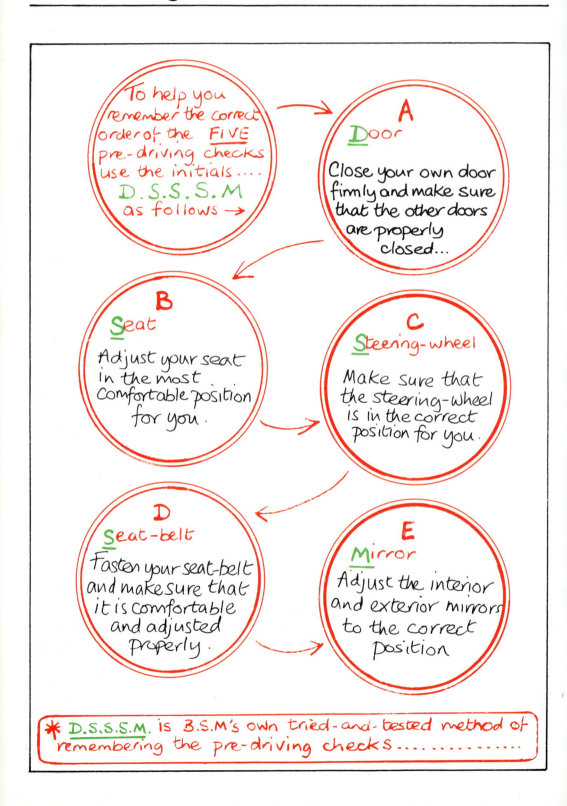

To help you remember the correct order of the **FIVE** pre-driving checks use the initials.... **D.S.S.S.M** as follows →

A

Door

Close your own door firmly and make sure that the other doors are properly closed...

B

Seat

Adjust your seat in the most comfortable position for you.

C

Steering-wheel

Make sure that the steering-wheel is in the correct position for you.

D

Seat-belt

Fasten your seat-belt and make sure that it is comfortable and adjusted properly.

E

Mirror

Adjust the interior and exterior mirrors to the correct position

***** **D.S.S.S.M.** is B.S.M's own tried-and-tested method of remembering the pre-driving checks.............

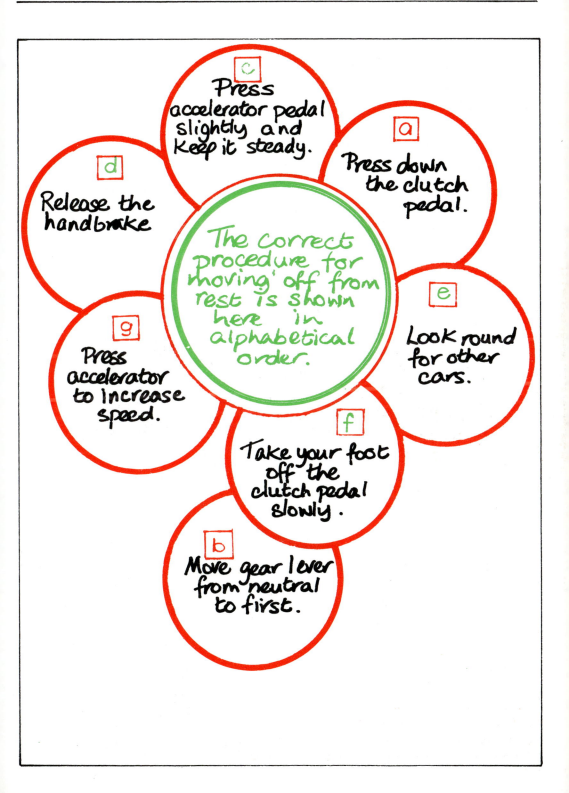

c Press accelerator pedal slightly and keep it steady.

a Press down the clutch pedal.

d Release the handbrake

The correct procedure for moving off from rest is shown here in alphabetical order.

e Look round for other cars.

g Press accelerator to increase speed.

f Take your foot off the clutch pedal slowly.

b Move gear lever from neutral to first.

The Stop sign

☑ ☐ b. You should
T F only enter the
main road when you can do so
without causing danger or
making drivers on that road change
speed or direction.

☐ ☒ C. T F
FALSE The two
solid lines at the
end of the road tell
you how far
forward you
should go.

☑ ☐
a. T F
Giving a signal,
getting into the
correct position,
and adjusting your
speed are all essential
to the right-
hand turn.

Here are
the answers
to the
TRUE / FALSE
questions about
turning right into
a main road.

☐ ☒
d. T F
FALSE You should
check your mirror
and look right, left, and
then right again before
emerging.

☑ ☐
e. T F
When it is safe to emerge
you should move off
smoothly and begin
your turn immediately
after passing the
centre of the road.

Stopping behind a parked car

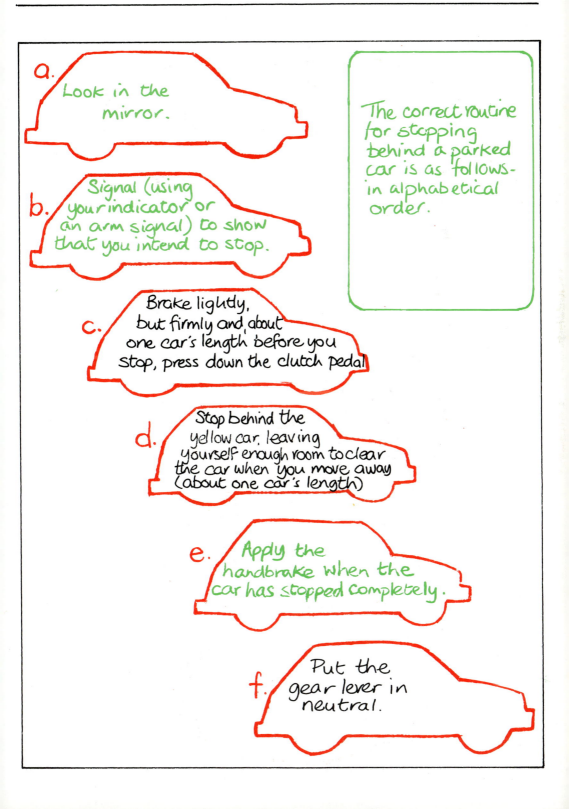

a. Look in the mirror.

The correct routine for stopping behind a parked car is as follows- in alphabetical order.

b. Signal (using your indicator or an arm signal) to show that you intend to stop.

c. Brake lightly, but firmly and, about one car's length before you stop, press down the clutch pedal

d. Stop behind the yellow car, leaving yourself enough room to clear the car when you move away (about one car's length)

e. Apply the handbrake when the car has stopped completely.

f. Put the gear lever in neutral.

5

Moving away at an angle

Your answers should be similar to these.........

a. What is the examiner looking for when he asks you to do this manoeuvre?

The examiner wants to make sure that you can move off safely at an angle from behind an obstruction (ie. the parked car.) This is a different test requirement than moving off straight ahead, which you already did at the Test Centre.

b. What two observational checks should you make before moving off?

Before moving off you should check for cars coming up from behind and for those approaching in the opposite direction.

c. There are two additional dangers that could occur in this situation—

What are they?

1. The person inside the yellow car might carelessly open the door.

2. The child by the lamp-post might walk out into the road. You might not be able to see her because your vision could be blocked by the yellow car.

d. How should you warn other vehicles that you intend to move off?

You should switch on your right indicator to warn other vehicles of your intentions.

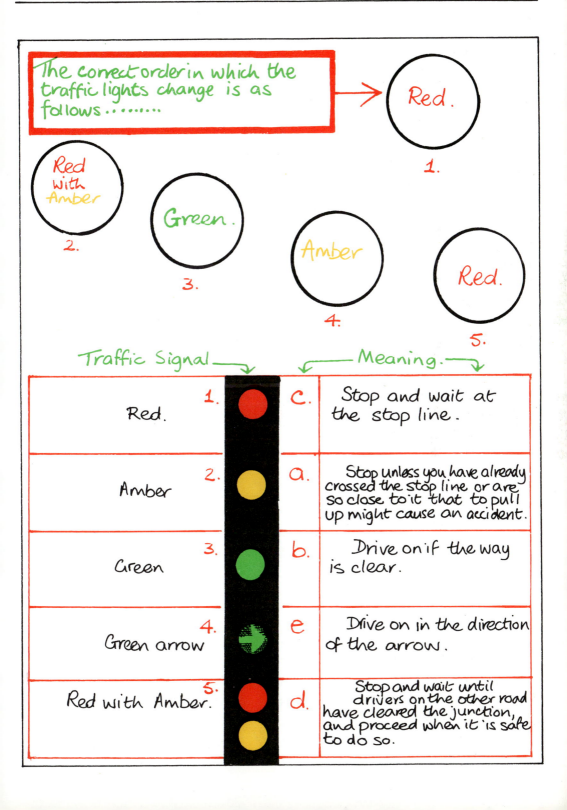

The correct order in which the traffic lights change is as follows ....

Red. 1.

Red with Amber 2.

Green. 3.

Amber 4.

Red. 5.

Traffic Signal

Meaning.

Traffic Signal			Meaning.
Red.	1.	c.	Stop and wait at the stop line.
Amber	2.	a.	Stop unless you have already crossed the stop line or are so close to it that to pull up might cause an accident.
Green	3.	b.	Drive on if the way is clear.
Green arrow	4.	e	Drive on in the direction of the arrow.
Red with Amber.	5.	d.	Stop and wait until drivers on the other road have cleared the junction, and proceed when it is safe to do so.

Turning left in a busy area

Overtaking a parked lorry

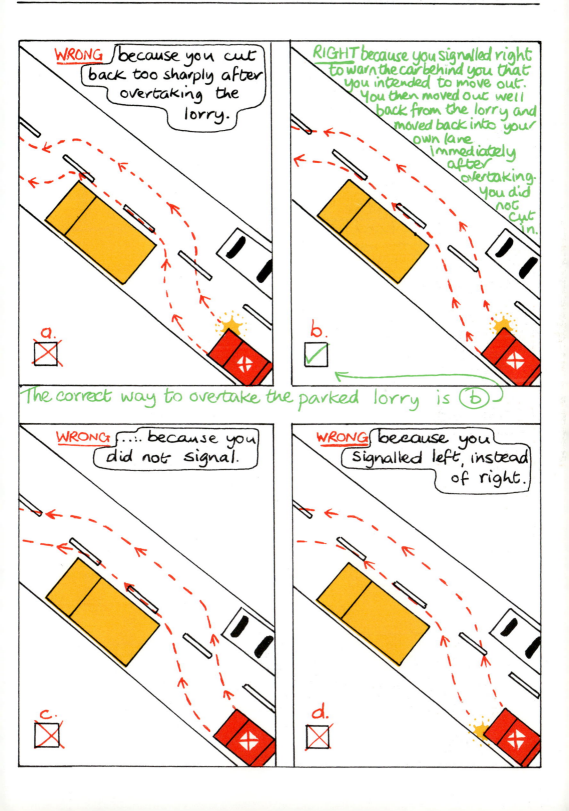

Turning right at a roundabout

d — Keep in the right-hand lane at the round-about

f — Change to signalling left when you pass the second exit.

a — Check your mirror.

The correct order of actions at the roundabout is shown alphabetically.

c — Give way to traffic approaching from the right at the roundabout

e — Check your mirror again

b — Put your right indicator on.

g — Take the third exit

The Emergency Stop

Here are the answers to the TRUE/FALSE questions about the Emergency Stop.

a FALSE because you do not need to make a special point of looking in your mirror.

T ◯ F ✓

b FALSE because you don't have to signal, it's more important to keep both hands on the wheel.

T ◯ F ✓

c TRUE You should gradually increase the pressure on the brake as you slow down, instead of stamping on it. Stamping hard on the brake can cause the wheels to lock and the car to skid out of control.

T ✓ F ◯

d FALSE because you should leave the clutch pedal alone until just before you stop. Being in gear will help to slow you down, assist you in braking and aid your stability.

T ◯ F ✓

e TRUE You should keep both hands on the steering-wheel until the car has stopped. This is because the car might veer slightly in one direction or the other and you must be in full control of the steering-wheel at all times.

T ✓ F ◯

f FALSE because you should leave your handbrake alone. Most handbrakes operate on the back wheels only, and if you put extra pressure on them you stand more chance of locking them and skidding.

T ◯ F ✓

g TRUE The amount of brake pressure you should apply depends on the state of the road surface. On wet or icy roads, for example, you must brake much more gently than on dry roads because your tyres will have less of a grip on the road.

T ✓ F ◯

Parking for the reverse

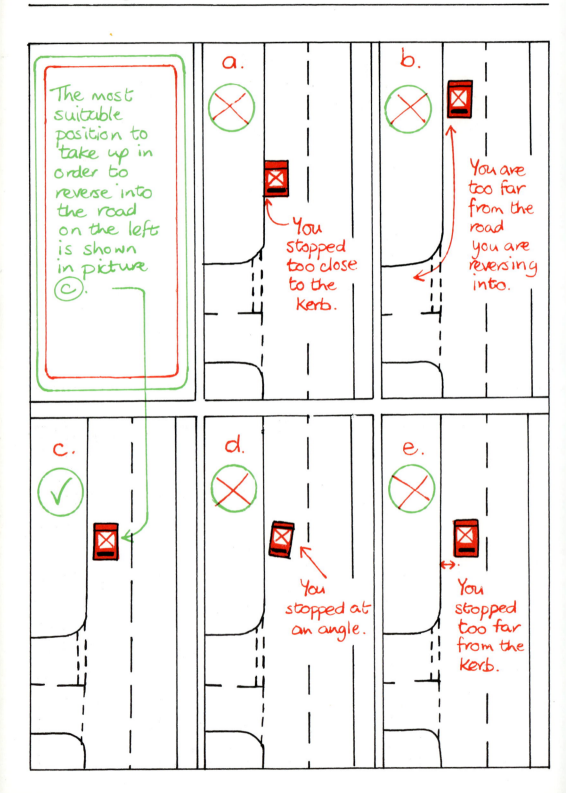

Reversing around a corner

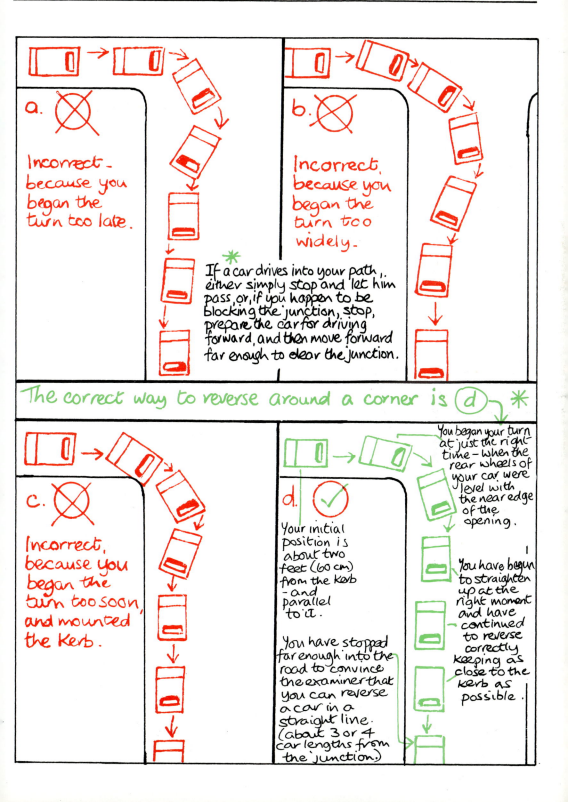

a. ⊗ Incorrect - because you began the turn too late.

b. ⊗ Incorrect, because you began the turn too widely.

※ If a car drives into your path, either simply stop and let him pass, or, if you happen to be blocking the junction, stop, prepare the car for driving forward, and then move forward far enough to clear the junction.

The correct way to reverse around a corner is (d) ※

c. ⊗ Incorrect, because you began the turn too soon, and mounted the kerb.

d. ✓ Your initial position is about two feet (60 cm) from the kerb - and parallel to it.

You have stopped far enough into the road to convince the examiner that you can reverse a car in a straight line. (about 3 or 4 car lengths from the junction.)

You began your turn at just the right time - when the rear wheels of your car were level with the near edge of the opening.

You have begun to straighten up at the right moment and have continued to reverse correctly keeping as close to the kerb as possible.

Turning left (after reverse)

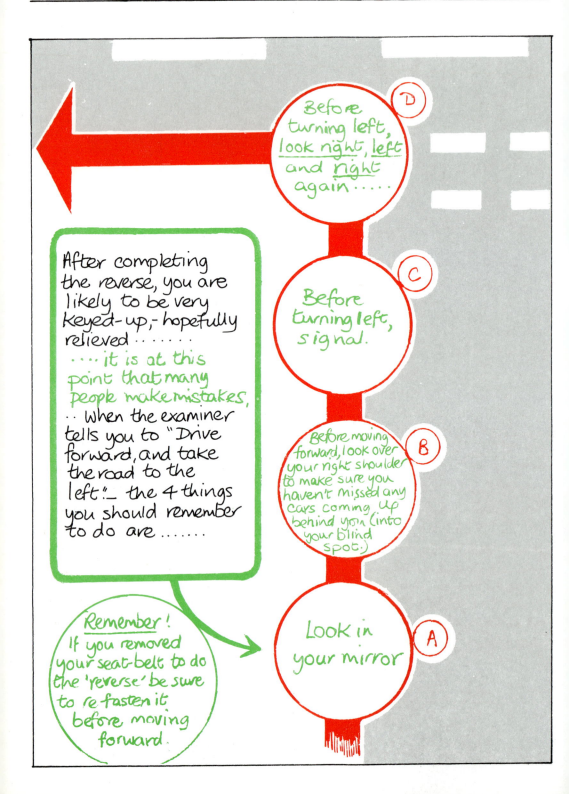

Judging a safe gap between cars

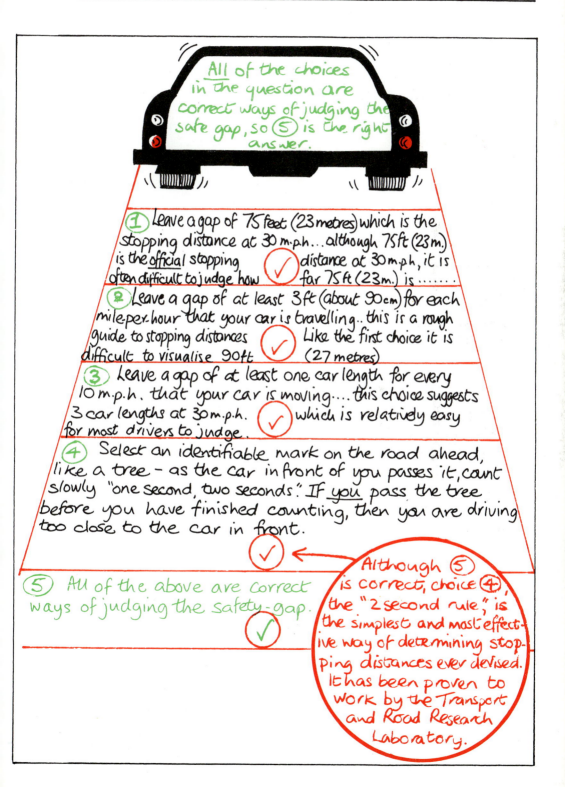

All of the choices in the question are correct ways of judging the safe gap, so ⑤ is the right answer.

① Leave a gap of 75 feet (23 metres) which is the stopping distance at 30 m.p.h...although 75ft (23m.) is the official stopping distance at 30m.p.h, it is often difficult to judge how ✓ far 75ft (23m.) is.......

② Leave a gap of at least 3ft (about 90cm) for each mile-per-hour that your car is travelling.. this is a rough guide to stopping distances Like the first choice it is difficult to visualise 90ft ✓ (27 metres)

③ Leave a gap of at least one car length for every 10 m.p.h. that your car is moving....this choice suggests 3 car lengths at 30m.p.h. ✓ which is relatively easy for most drivers to judge.

④ Select an identifiable mark on the road ahead, like a tree - as the car in front of you passes it, count slowly "one second, two seconds." If you pass the tree before you have finished counting, then you are driving too close to the car in front.

✓ ←

⑤ All of the above are correct ways of judging the safety-gap.

✓

Although ⑤ is correct, choice ④, the "2 second rule," is the simplest and most effective way of determining stopping distances ever devised. It has been proven to work by the Transport and Road Research Laboratory.

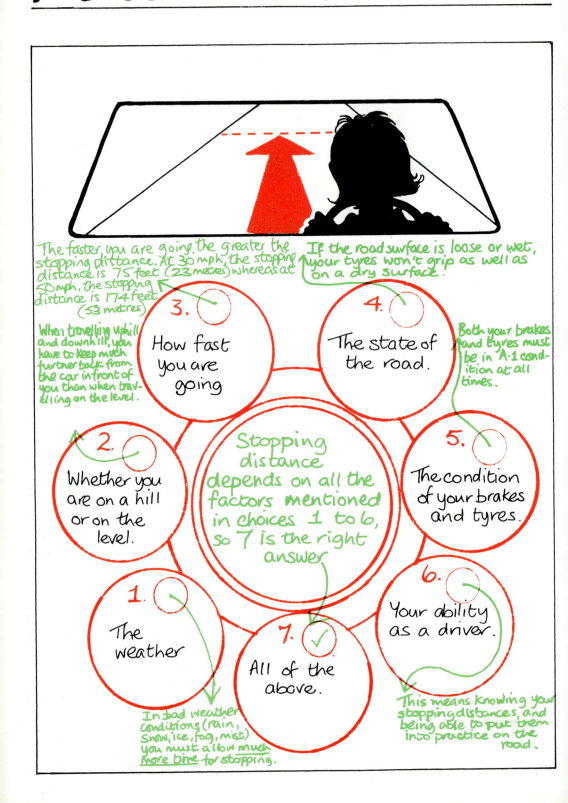

The faster you are going, the greater the stopping distance. At 30 mph, the stopping distance is 75 feet (23 metres) whereas at 50 mph, the stopping distance is 174 feet (53 metres)

If the road surface is loose or wet, your tyres won't grip as well as on a dry surface!

When travelling uphill and downhill, you have to keep much further back from the car in front of you than when travelling on the level.

3.
How fast you are going

4.
The state of the road.

Both your brakes and tyres must be in A·1 condition at all times.

2.
Whether you are on a hill or on the level.

Stopping distance depends on all the factors mentioned in choices 1 to 6, so 7 is the right answer

5.
The condition of your brakes and tyres.

1.
The weather

7. ✓
All of the above.

6.
Your ability as a driver.

In bad weather conditions (rain, snow, ice, fog, mist) you must allow much more time for stopping.

This means knowing your stopping distances, and being able to put them into practice on the road.

Overtaking parked cars

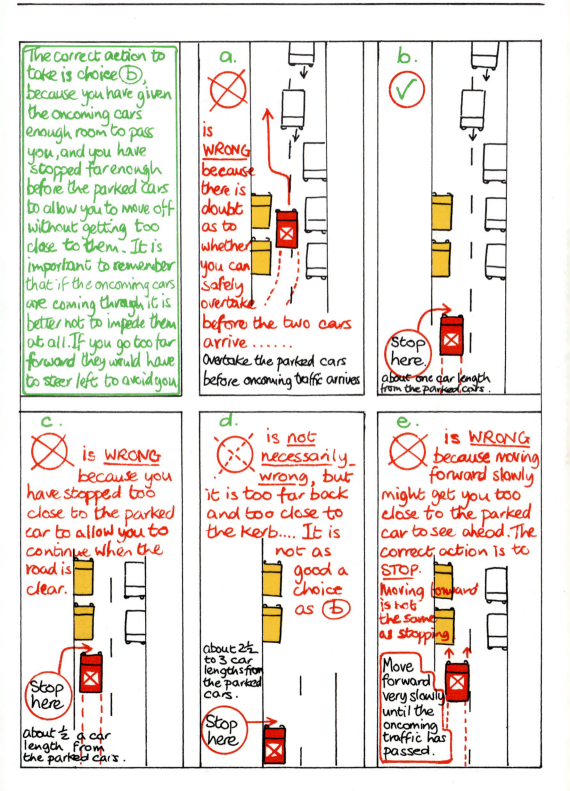

The correct action to take is choice ⓑ, because you have given the oncoming cars enough room to pass you, and you have stopped far enough before the parked cars to allow you to move off without getting too close to them. It is important to remember that if the oncoming cars are coming through it is better not to impede them at all. If you go too far forward they would have to steer left to avoid you.

a. ⊗ is WRONG because there is doubt as to whether you can safely overtake before the two cars arrive ......
Overtake the parked cars before oncoming traffic arrives

b. ✓
Stop here.
about one car length from the parked cars.

c. ⊗ is WRONG because you have stopped too close to the parked car to allow you to continue when the road is clear.
Stop here
about ½ a car length from the parked cars.

d. ⊗ is not necessarily wrong, but it is too far back and too close to the kerb.... It is not as good a choice as ⓑ
about 2½ to 3 car lengths from the parked cars.
Stop here

e. ⊗ is WRONG because moving forward slowly might get you too close to the parked car to see ahead. The correct action is to STOP. Moving forward is not the same as stopping
Move forward very slowly until the oncoming traffic has passed.

Going uphill

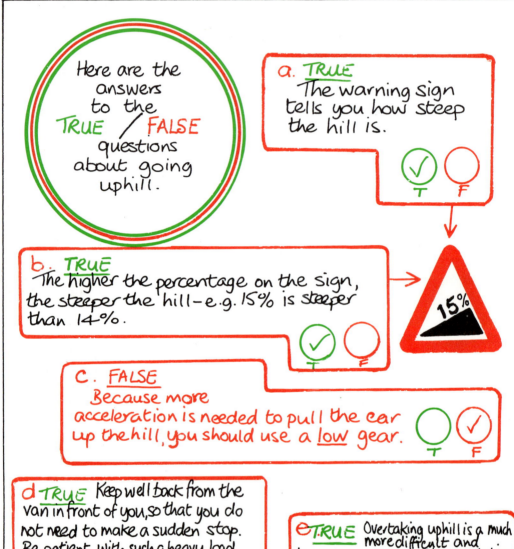

Here are the answers to the TRUE / FALSE questions about going uphill.

a. TRUE
The warning sign tells you how steep the hill is.

T ✓ F

b. TRUE
The higher the percentage on the sign, the steeper the hill – e.g. 15% is steeper than 14%.

T ✓ F

c. FALSE
Because more acceleration is needed to pull the car up the hill, you should use a low gear.

T F ✓

d TRUE Keep well back from the van in front of you, so that you do not need to make a sudden stop. Be patient with such a heavy load, the driver of the van will find it very difficult to change gears and maintain a sufficient road speed.

T ✓ F

e TRUE Overtaking uphill is a much more difficult and dangerous manoeuvre than overtaking on the level. This is because you need more speed and more time to overtake vehicles uphill. The big danger is that a vehicle coming towards you downhill will often be moving much faster than you realise and will, therefore, require much more time to slow down.

T ✓ F

Moving off uphill

You should have filled in the blanks with answers like these—

(a) The main difference between starting off uphill and on the level road is that slightly more {power/acceleration} is necessary on the hill start.

(b) Because your car will be slower in moving away uphill and gaining speed than on the level, you will need to find a larger gap in the traffic if you are to fit in safely.

(c) If your handbrake is released before the clutch is at the point of contact, then the car will roll backwards

(d) It is important not to bring the clutch up any higher than the point of contact because your car would try to move forward before you release the handbrake and you would stall

(e) Before moving off remember to :
(i) Look in your mirror.
(ii) Look over your right shoulder.
(iii) Look at the road ahead.
(iv) Check your mirror again.
(v) Signal right.

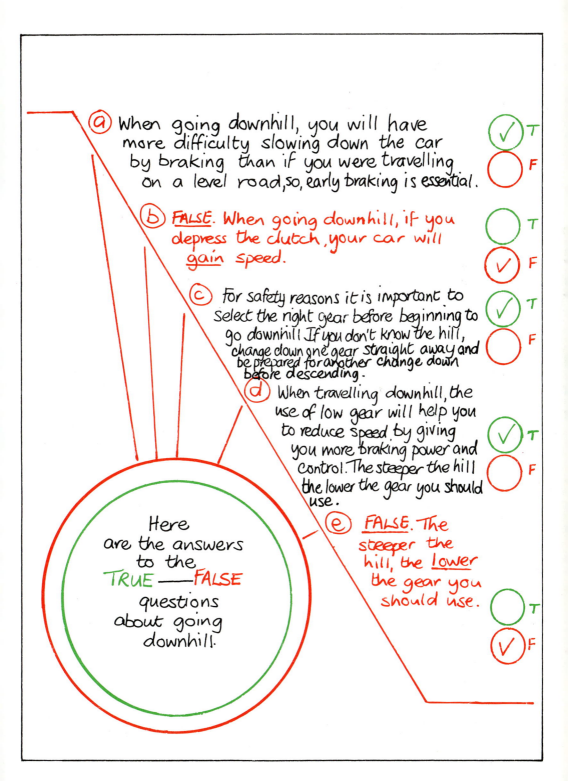

(a) When going downhill, you will have more difficulty slowing down the car by braking than if you were travelling on a level road, so, early braking is essential. ✓ T ○ F

(b) FALSE. When going downhill, if you depress the clutch, your car will gain speed. ○ T ✓ F

(c) For safety reasons it is important to select the right gear before beginning to go downhill. If you don't know the hill, change down one gear straight away and be prepared for another change down before descending. ✓ T ○ F

(d) When travelling downhill, the use of low gear will help you to reduce speed by giving you more braking power and control. The steeper the hill the lower the gear you should use. ✓ T ○ F

(e) FALSE. The steeper the hill, the lower the gear you should use. ○ T ✓ F

Here are the answers to the TRUE——FALSE questions about going downhill.

Approaching a pedestrian crossing

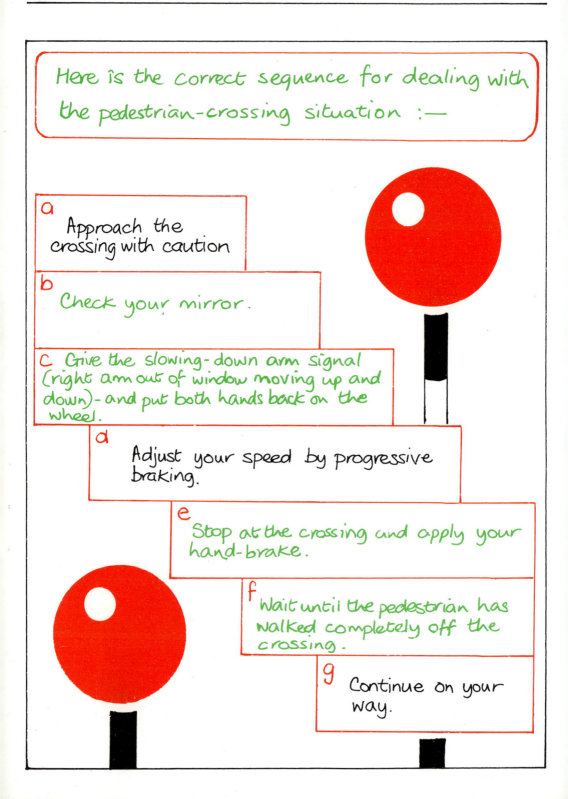

Here is the correct sequence for dealing with the pedestrian-crossing situation :—

a Approach the crossing with caution

b Check your mirror.

c Give the slowing-down arm signal (right arm out of window moving up and down)-and put both hands back on the wheel.

d Adjust your speed by progressive braking.

e Stop at the crossing and apply your hand-brake.

f Wait until the pedestrian has walked completely off the crossing.

g Continue on your way.

Parking for turning in the road

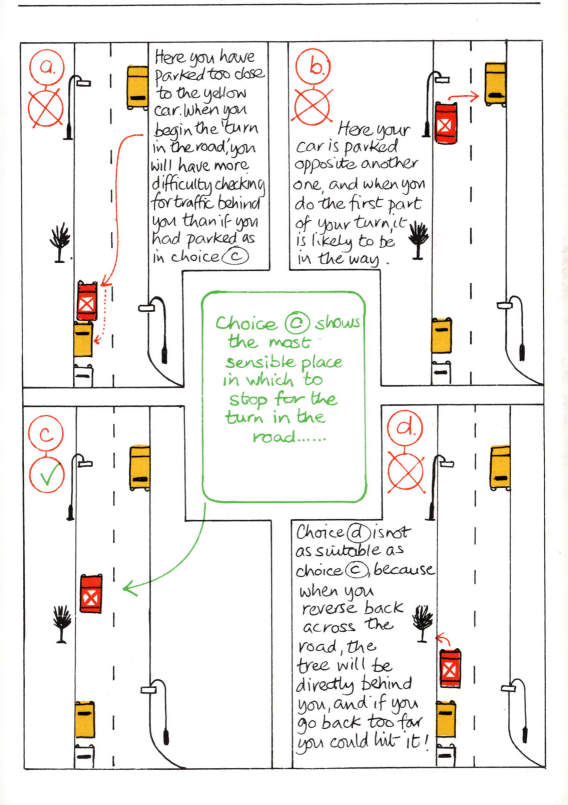

a. Here you have parked too close to the yellow car. When you begin the 'turn in the road', you will have more difficulty checking for traffic behind you than if you had parked as in choice ©

b. Here your car is parked opposite another one, and when you do the first part of your turn, it is likely to be in the way.

Choice © shows the most sensible place in which to stop for the turn in the road......

c. ✓

d. Choice ⓓ is not as suitable as choice ©, because when you reverse back across the road, the tree will be directly behind you, and if you go back too far you could hit it!

Turning in the road

The correct steps for turning in the road are given below..

(Make sure that your car does not move until full observations have been completed....)

a. Select first gear, press the accelerator lightly, and release the hand-brake.

b. Make sure that it is safe to move off by checking ① your mirror ② over your right shoulder ③ the road ahead. ④ Your mirror again.

c. Bring the clutch up slowly until the car begins to move and then steer quickly and fully to the right.

d. When you're over the centre of the road, push the clutch down, steer to the left and, when you are near to the kerb gently brake to stop

e. Remembering that the car will be on a slope, prepare for moving back across the road in the same way as you would prepare the car for a hill-start.

f. Check that it is safe to move back across the road, by ① looking right, left, and over your left shoulder for pedestrians; ② prepare the car for moving off by balancing the car on the clutch and releasing the handbrake ③ then do your observations by looking right, left and right again

g. When the car begins to move, steer to the left

h. When you're over the centre of the road, push the clutch down steer right and when you are near to the kerb gently brake to stop.

i. Prepare the car for moving forward by
① looking in your mirror.
② looking right, left, and right again
③ looking at the road ahead, slowly move forward to a parking position.

This manoeuvre is often referred to as the '3-point turn'- however it is not essential that you complete the turn in the road in 3 movements. You may take 5 or even 7 movements depending on the size of your car, its steering circle and the width of the road.

Making progress to suit road conditions

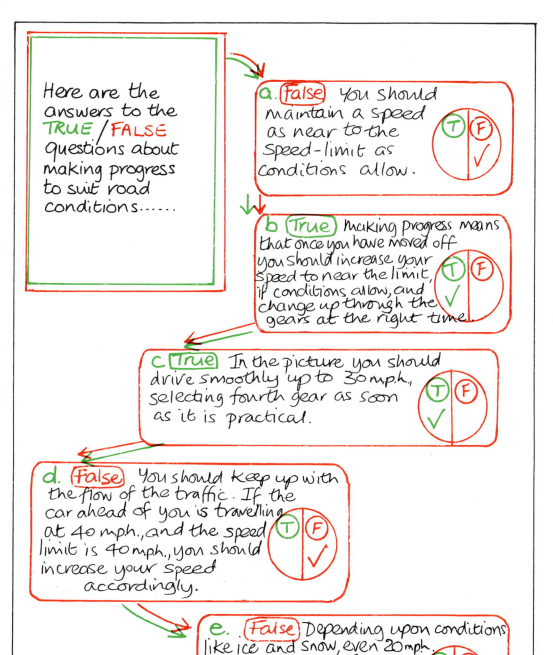

Here are the answers to the TRUE / FALSE questions about making progress to suit road conditions......

a. false You should maintain a speed as near to the speed-limit as conditions allow.

T F ✓

b. True making progress means that once you have moved off you should increase your speed to near the limit, if conditions allow, and change up through the gears at the right time.

T F ✓

c. True In the picture you should drive smoothly up to 30 m.p.h., selecting fourth gear as soon as it is practical.

T F ✓

d. False You should keep up with the flow of the traffic. If the car ahead of you is travelling at 40 mph., and the speed limit is 40 mph., you should increase your speed accordingly.

T F ✓

e. False Depending upon conditions like ice and snow, even 20 mph. can be dangerous. Travelling too slowly can also hold up other traffic and cause traffic congestion.

T F ✓

Approaching crossroads

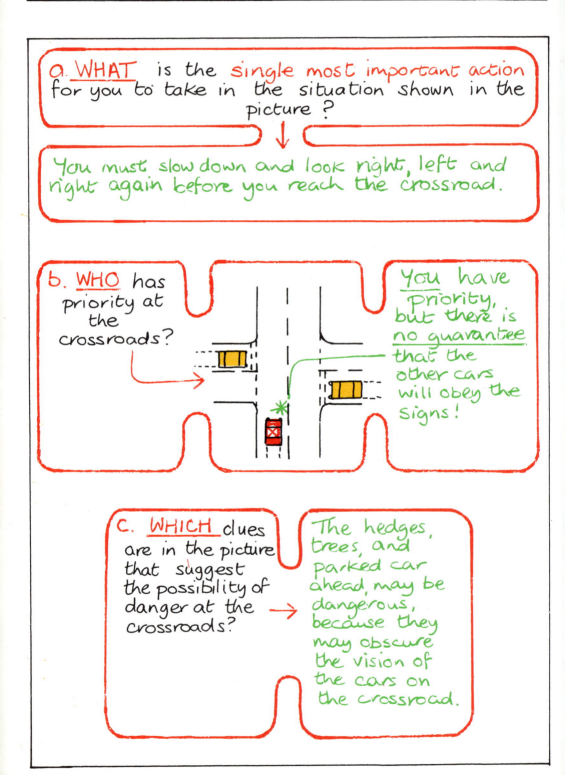

a. <u>WHAT</u> is the single most important action for you to take in the situation shown in the picture?

↓

You must slow down and look right, left and right again before you reach the crossroad.

b. <u>WHO</u> has priority at the crossroads?

You have priority, but there is no guarantee that the other cars will obey the signs!

c. <u>WHICH</u> clues are in the picture that suggest the possibility of danger at the crossroads?

The hedges, trees, and parked car ahead, may be dangerous, because they may obscure the vision of the cars on the crossroad.

A dangerous situation

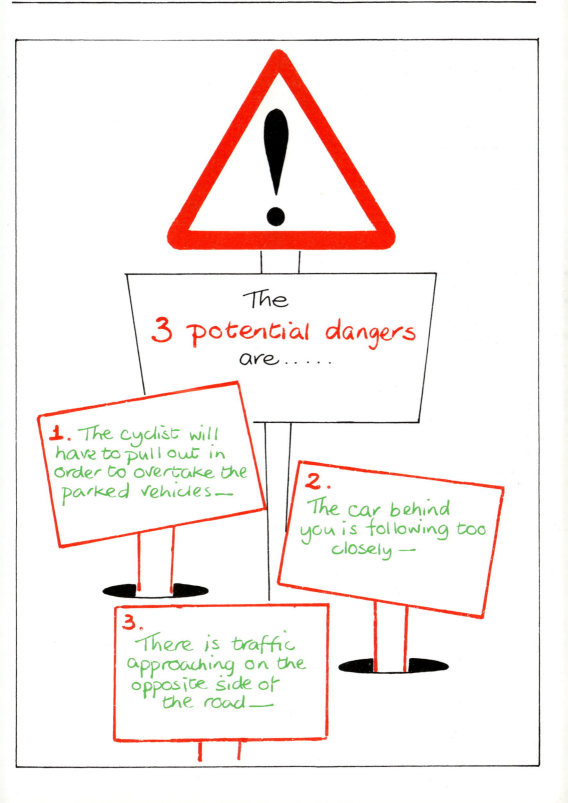

The Double Bend

Your answers should be similar to these ......

a. What does the sign indicate?

The sign indicates that you are approaching a double bend, first to the right, and then to the left.

b. ① is correct, because it is well to the left of the road. Because your view of the road ahead will be restricted, you should slow down. Your speed should be lowest just as you begin to take the bend.

② is wrong →

—because you are too close to the centre of the road and therefore, closer to any approaching traffic. This gives you less of a safety margin, particularly if a vehicle coming towards you is very close to the centre line.

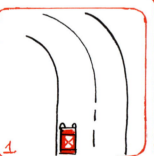

1

2

c. The 2 continuous white lines mean that:

You must <u>not</u> cross them.

d. The broken lines between the 2 bends indicate that

You may cross <u>if it is safe</u> to do so.

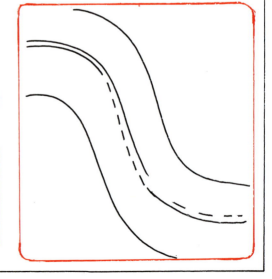

Level crossing – half-barriers

a. What do the amber lights and flashing red lights mean?

→ The first warning that a train is coming.

b. What will happen within seconds when the red lights begin to flash?

→ The barriers will come down across half the road.

c. What should you do when the barriers come down?

→ Stop as close to the stop-line as possible.

d. What should you do if you are crossing the tracks and you hear the bells begin to ring?

Keep going over the crossing.....

e. What should you do if you stall on the crossing?

You and the examiner should get out of the car and clear of the crossing – then 'phone the signalman immediately.

Give-way sign at a T-junction

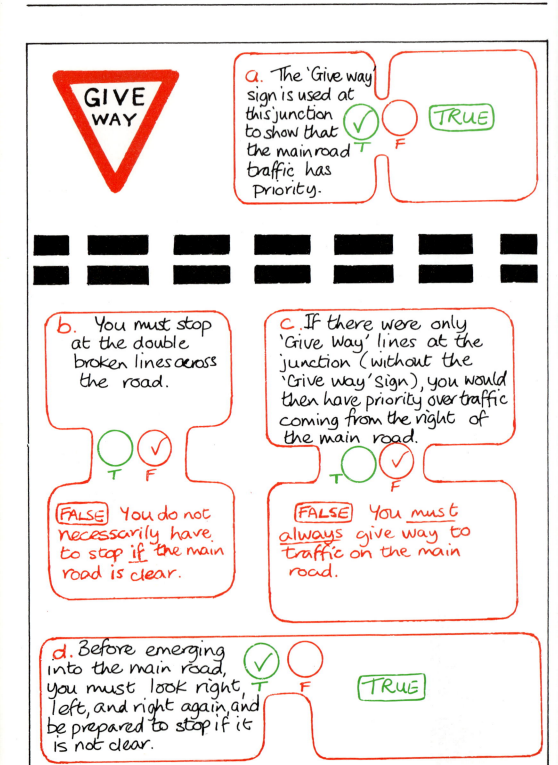

GIVE WAY

a. The 'Give way' sign is used at this junction to show that the main road traffic has priority.
✓ T   F   TRUE

b. You must stop at the double broken lines across the road.
T   ✓ F
FALSE You do not necessarily have to stop if the main road is clear.

c. If there were only 'Give Way' lines at the junction (without the 'Give way' sign), you would then have priority over traffic coming from the right of the main road.
T   ✓ F
FALSE You must always give way to traffic on the main road.

d. Before emerging into the main road, you must look right, left, and right again, and be prepared to stop if it is not clear.
✓ T   F   TRUE

The staggered junction

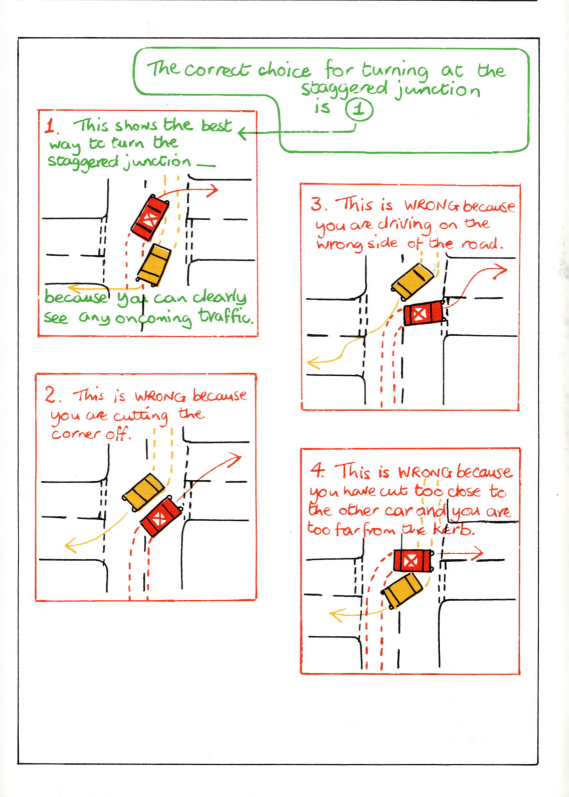

Straight on at a roundabout

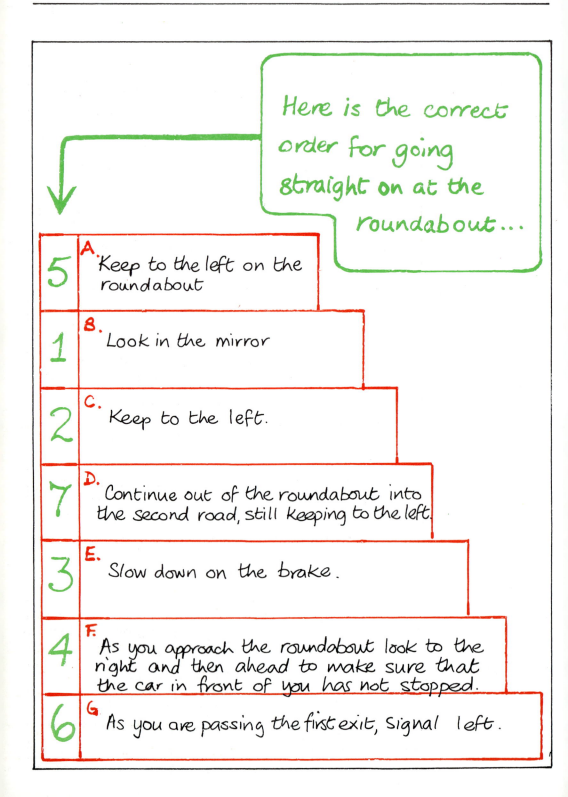

Here is the correct order for going straight on at the roundabout...

5   **A.** Keep to the left on the roundabout

1   **B.** Look in the mirror

2   **C.** Keep to the left.

7   **D.** Continue out of the roundabout into the second road, still keeping to the left.

3   **E.** Slow down on the brake.

4   **F.** As you approach the roundabout look to the right and then ahead to make sure that the car in front of you has not stopped.

6   **G.** As you are passing the first exit, signal left.

Turning right off a dual carriageway

Here are the correct steps for turning right off a dual carriageway.

A ↳ X Look in the mirror and slow down.

Should be

✓ Look in the mirror **without** slowing down

B ↳ X Signal right only when it is safe to move over to the right-hand lane.

Should be

✓ Signal right even if it is not immediately safe to move over to the right-hand lane (because this gives other vehicles due warning of your intention)

C ↳ X Move over to the right-hand lane when you are about 10 feet (3 metres) from the junction.

Should be

✓ Move over to the right-hand lane when it is safe to do so.

D ↳ ✓ Slow down by braking and change to a lower gear ready for your turn.

↳ is a correct statement.

E ↓ X When you reach the central reservation, turn your indicator off and wait until it is safe to make your turn.

Should be

✓ When you reach the central reservation, stop and wait until it is safe to cross and make your turn. (Keep your right indicator on.)

The One-way street

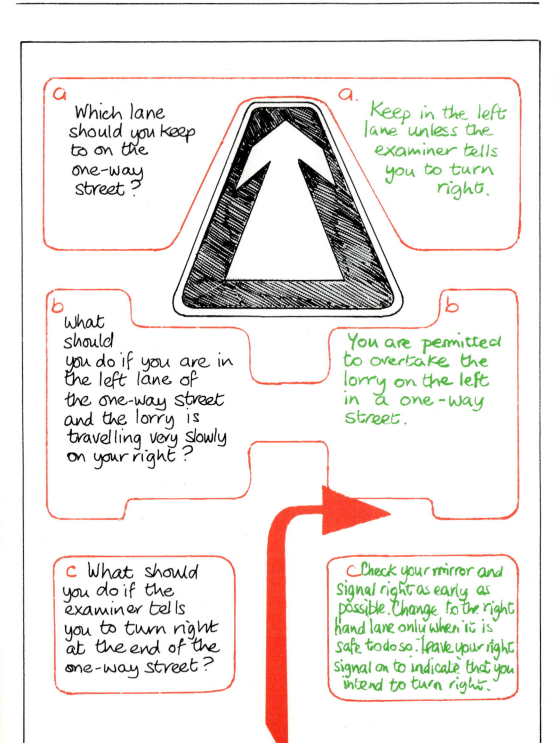

a Which lane should you keep to on the one-way street?

a. Keep in the left lane unless the examiner tells you to turn right.

b What should you do if you are in the left lane of the one-way street and the lorry is travelling very slowly on your right?

b You are permitted to overtake the lorry on the left in a one-way street.

c What should you do if the examiner tells you to turn right at the end of the one-way street?

c Check your mirror and signal right as early as possible. Change to the right hand lane only when it is safe to do so. Leave your right signal on to indicate that you intend to turn right.

Green filter traffic-lights

a
Wrong You do not have to wait at the stop-line if you are turning left and the filter-arrow is green.

b
Wrong You do not have to wait at the stop-line if you are turning left and the filter-arrow is green.

Choice 'c' is correct

e
Wrong The green filter arrow means that you can proceed without stopping if it is safe to do so.

c
Correct The green filter arrow tells you that you can turn left without stopping if it is safe to do so.

d
Wrong You do not even need to stop briefly at the lights.

The pelican-crossing

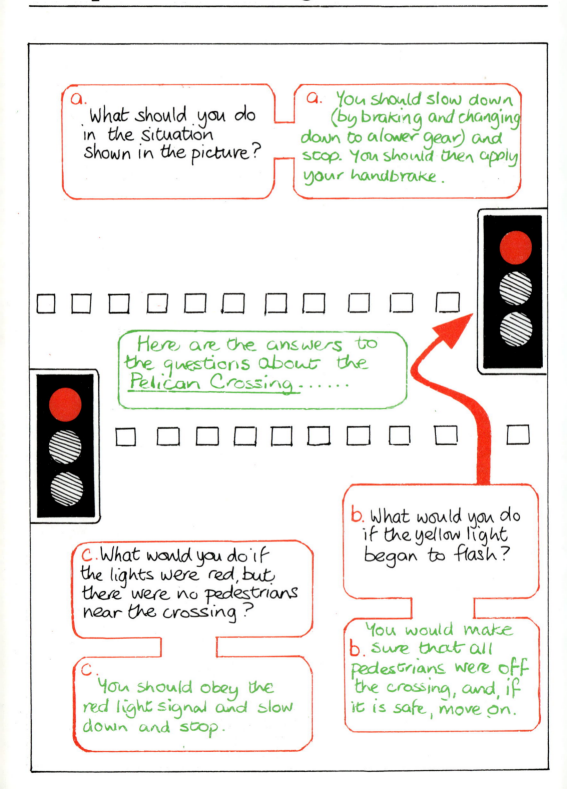

a. What should you do in the situation shown in the picture?

a. You should slow down (by braking and changing down to a lower gear) and stop. You should then apply your handbrake.

Here are the answers to the questions about the Pelican Crossing......

b. What would you do if the yellow light began to flash?

c. What would you do if the lights were red, but there were no pedestrians near the crossing?

c. You should obey the red light signal and slow down and stop.

b. You would make sure that all pedestrians were off the crossing, and, if it is safe, move on.

a

What should you do when you arrive at the box-junction, if you are going straight on?

a

When you arrive at the box-junction, you do not enter it until
· your way through it is clear — and
· your exit (i.e. the road ahead) is clear.

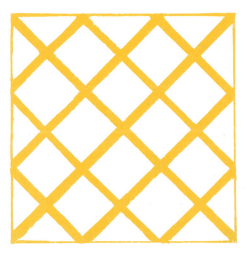

b.

What should you do when you arrive at the box-junction, if you want to turn right and there is a steady stream of traffic coming towards you?

b. When you arrive at the box-junction you must determine whether your exit (ie the road you are turning right into) is clear. If it is you are permitted to enter the box-junction and wait there for a safe gap in the traffic. If your exit is not clear, you are not permitted to enter the box-junction.

The mini-roundabout

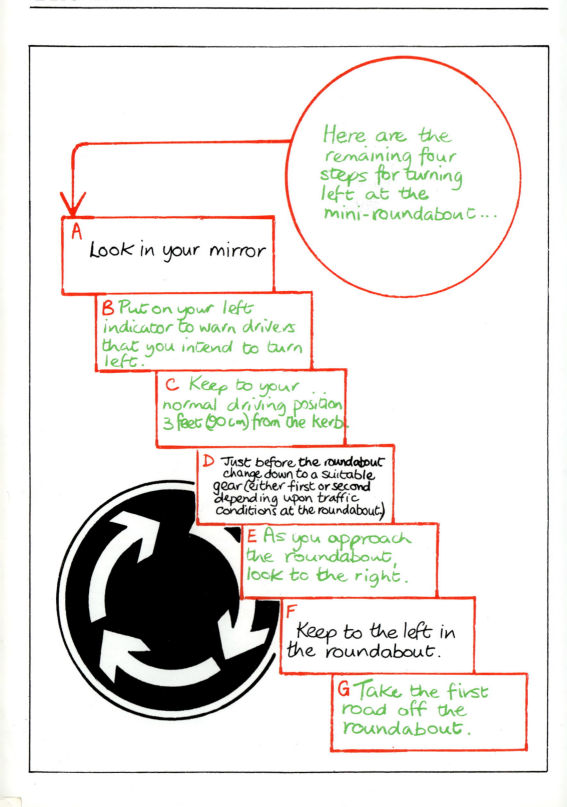

Here are the remaining four steps for turning left at the mini-roundabout...

A Look in your mirror

B Put on your left indicator to warn drivers that you intend to turn left.

C Keep to your normal driving position 3 feet (90 cm) from the kerb.

D Just before the roundabout change down to a suitable gear (either first or second depending upon traffic conditions at the roundabout.)

E As you approach the roundabout, look to the right.

F Keep to the left in the roundabout.

G Take the first road off the roundabout.

Stopping behind a bus

This is the best place for you to stop because it is far enough back for you to see round the bus. If the bus remains there a while, you may have to overtake it, and if you are too close, it will be impossible to see.

Turning right (from a major to minor road

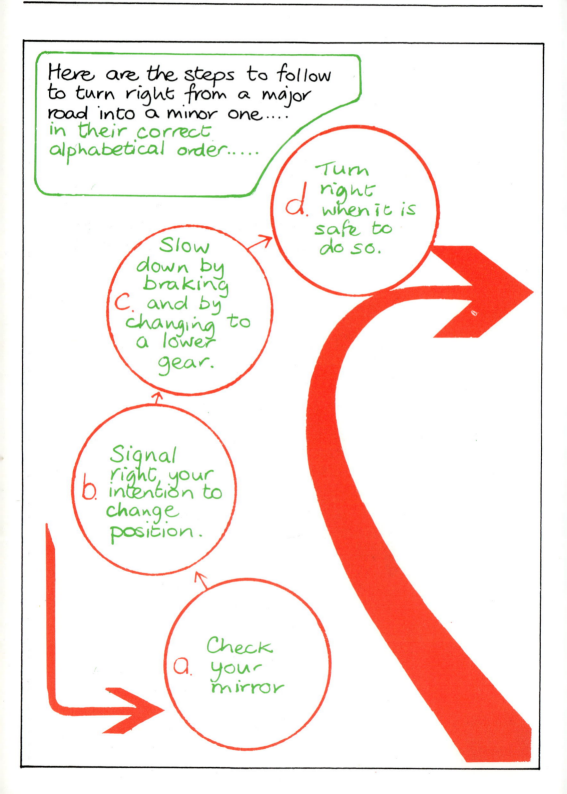

Parking in a limited space

The correct procedure for parking in a limited space is shown here in alphabetical order.

(E) When the front of your car has cleared the rear of the forward parked car, turn the wheel briskly to the right.

(G) If necessary move forward to straighten up.

(A) Stop your car when your rear bumper is halfway along the front car and about 3 feet (90 cm) out from it.

(F) Continue reversing slowly and straighten your wheel as necessary.

(D) Aim for the nearside front corner of the rear parked car.

(C) Reverse until you are alongside the front car, and then steer left.

(B) Before reversing look all around you to make sure it is safe.

Highway Code Answers

1. Assume you are driving on a three-lane motorway at 70 m.p.h. and there are no other vehicles near you. Which lane should you be in?

You should be in the left-hand lane. That is your normal driving position when there is no traffic. If there are many slow moving vehicles in the left lane, you may stay in the middle lane. The right-hand lane is for overtaking.

2. What is the meaning of a red warning sign (a reflecting triangle) placed on the road?

The red triangle is a warning sign that there is an accident or an obstruction ahead.

3. What should you do if you are travelling along a country road during the day, and you enter a fog?

You should turn your headlamps and rearlamps on and observe the Fog Code (eg. slow down, keep a safe distance from the car in front. Make sure you can pull up within your range of vision, use windscreen wipers if necessary. Allow more time for your journey.

4. Under what circumstances should you flash your head-lamps?

You should only flash your headlamps to let another driver know you are there.

5. What do these traffic signs mean?

a. No left turn.

b. Slippery road.

c. Falling or fallen rocks.

6. What do these traffic signs mean?

a. No overtaking

b. Traffic merges from left.

c. Uneven road.

Highway Code Answers

Set II

1. Which lane on the motorway is the acceleration-lane?

The acceleration lane is the extra lane on the side of the motorway that allows you to adjust your speed when joining the motorway. It is the continuation of the slip road on the left that you use to enter the motorway.

2. What is the ideal distance for stopping behind another car at a stop sign?

The ideal distance for stopping behind another car is half-a-car length behind it.

3. What should you do if you are travelling along a dual carriageway during the daytime and it begins to rain very heavily?

You should turn on your headlamps and rearlamps, slow down, keep well back from the car ahead of you, make sure you can pull up within the range of your vision, brake more gently because your tyres won't grip the road very well, and allow more time for your journey.

4. When is it an offence to sound your horn?

When you are moving it is an offence to sound your horn in a built-up area between the hours of 11.30 pm and 7 am. When your car is stationary, it is an offence to sound your horn except to warn a moving vehicle of danger.

5. What do these traffic-signs mean?

a. No U-turns.

b. No entry for vehicular traffic.

c. Road narrows on both sides of the road.

6. What do these traffic-signs mean?

a No vehicles over heights shown (14'.6")

b. Right-hand lane closed.

c. Opening or swing bridge ahead.

Highway Code Answers

Set III ─ ─ ─ ─ ─ ─ ─ ─ ─ ─ ─ ─ ─ ─ ─ ─ ─ ─ ─ ✳ ✳ ✳

1. When driving on a motorway at night, you will see (a) amber-coloured studs (b) red studs (c) green studs – What does each type of coloured stud mean?

(a) amber studs mark the right hand edge of the motorway. (b) Red studs mark the left hand edge. (c) Green studs divide the acceleration and deceleration lanes from the through carriageways.

2. What should you do if you are travelling downhill on a single-track road and a car is approaching uphill?

You should give way to vehicles coming up-hill on single-track roads, whenever possible.

3. Can you name two causes of skidding?

Skidding can be caused in wet or icy conditions by quick, hard braking, suddenly accelerating, or turning the steering wheel too quickly.

4. When are you permitted to use a hazard-warning device? (ie. the switch which causes all of your indicators to flash at the same time.)

You are permitted to use a hazard-warning light when your vehicle is stationary, to indicate that it is causing a temporary obstruction to the flow of traffic (e.g. because you have broken down or are loading or unloading)

✳ You must never use the hazard device when you are moving.

5. What do these traffic signs mean?

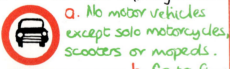

a. No motor vehicles except solo motorcycles, scooters or mopeds.

b. Contra-flow bus lane (bus lane against traffic.)

c. Location of level-crossing without barrier or gate.

6. What do these traffic signs mean?

a. Give priority to vehicles from opposite direction.

b. Change to opposite carriageway.

c. "Count-down" markers approaching concealed level-crossing.

Driver's Score Card

No.	Situation	Pass	Fail
1.	Pre-driving check.		
2	Moving off from rest.		
3	The Stop sign.		
4	Stopping behind a parked car		
5	Moving away at an angle.		
6	Traffic-light signals.		
7	Turning left in a busy area.		
8	Overtaking a parked lorry.		
9	Turning right at a roundabout.		
10	The Emergency Stop.		
11	Parking for the reverse.		
12	Reversing around a corner.		
13	Turning left (after reverse)		
14	Judging a safe gap between cars.		
15	Judging your stopping distance		
16	Overtaking parked cars.		
17	Going uphill.		
	Sub-total.		

Driver's Score Card

No.	Situation.	Pass	Fail
18	Stopping on hills.		
19	Moving off uphill.		
20	Going downhill.		
21	Approaching a pedestrian crossing.		
22	Parking for turning in the road.		
23	Turning in the road.		
24	Making progress to suit road conditions.		
25	Approaching crossroads.		
26	A dangerous situation.		
27	The Double Bend.		
28	Level-crossing – half-barriers		
29	Give-way sign at a T-junction.		
30	The staggered junction		
31	Straight on at a roundabout		
32	Turning right off a dual carriageway.		
	Sub-total.		
	Sub-total from previous page		
	Total so far.		

Driver's Score Card

No.	Situation Score needed.	Pass	Fail
33	The One-way street.		
34	Green filter traffic-lights.		
35	The pelican-crossing		
36	The Box-junction		
37	The mini-roundabout.		
38	Stopping behind a Bus.		
39	Turning right (from a major to minor road)		
40	Parking in a limited space.		
1.	Highway Code Questions. (any set)		
2.	∗ ∗∗ ∗∗∗		
3.	∗ ∗ ∗ ∗∗∗		
4.	∗ ∗∗ ∗∗ ∗		
5.	∗ ∗ ∗ ∗∗∗		
6.	∗ ∗ ∗ ∗ ∗∗		
	Sub- total		
	Total from previous page		
	and here is your final score →		

Now turn the page
to discover whether you are ready for your Driving Test →

Are you ready for your Driving Test?

If you scored 36 or more, congratulations! You are ready to take your driving test.

GOOD LUCK!

If you scored between 30 and 35, you are nearly there. Use the Driver's Score Card to spot your weaknesses, and re-read the appropriate parts of the Highway Code and the booklet "How to Pass Your Driving Test" then try to answer the questions again to see if your score goes up to 36.

If you scored 29 or less, you are not ready to take your test. Show your scorecard to your driving instructor and decide on a positive plan of action. Then, try the questions again to see how much you have improved.